# Science in the Bible

# Science in the Bible

How Biblical Writers
Viewed Science

**Acknowledgements**

Except where noted, Scriptures taken from the Holy Bible are the New International Version®, NIV®. Copyright © 1973, 1978, 1984, 2011 by Biblica, Inc.™ Used by permission of Zondervan. All rights reserved worldwide. www.zondervan.com. The "NIV" and "New International Version" are trademarks registered in the United States Patent and Trademark Office by Biblica, Inc.™

To emphasize particular points I have put in bold certain words of the quoted scriptures. These are my additions and not in the original Bible translation.

**Dedicated to the memory of Paul Vander Kooi**

# Contents

# Science in the Bible

# Preface

Our understanding of the world is different from that of the writers of the Bible.  As an example, we know that the earth is a sphere; they did not. The first reason I wrote these essays was that I was curious whether we would get more insight into the Truths of the Bible if we knew what writers were thinking about the natural world.

Another reason to look into the scientific thought of the Bible is that, in many people's minds, there is a conflict between science and religion. I want to show that writers of the Bible were interested in the natural world and they used the best information on science and technology that they had at the time of writing. If they used the best scientific knowledge at the time, do you think it is OK for us to do that too?

Finally, if we understand the relationship between the natural world and the scriptures we might think about our relationship to God more often.  Genesis 9:13, the symbol of the rainbow seen by Noah after the flood is explicitly used as a covenant:

*[13] I have set my rainbow in the clouds, and it will be the sign of the covenant between me and the earth.*

Other natural phenomena were both explicitly and implicitly used to explain religious principles. The first two chapters describes how wind and fire were used to describe the Holy Spirit. Subsequent chapters describe how scientific understanding in Biblical times of water and food affected the sacraments of Baptism and Communion. The stories of creation in Genesis are compared with scientific view of the origin of life. Diseases perplex us today as they did in ancient times, and we still suffer from infectious diseases and diseases of nutrition. Light and vision was seen differently from what we think of them now. Ultimately, we, like the Bible writers, must acknowledge that we only can marvel of the grandeur of the universe and God's creation.

The seed for this book came from my brother, Paul Vander Kooi. He once said to me that in all cases the writers of the Bible used the best available scientific knowledge to write about their understanding of God. Unfortunately, he is no longer with us. I like to think that he would have approved at what I wrote, although I think he would have had insights that I missed.

I thank my family members who are related to me and those who are part of my extended family through love and affection.  John Vander Kooi, Carl Vander Kooi, Lois Vander Kooi, Ruth Vander Kooi, Maria Erecinska, Ian Silver, Lori Geres and Jane Ormsby all gave valuable criticisms and suggestions. They did not always agree with what I wrote; all mistakes in the book are solely attributed to me. I talked with Pastor John Buechner about the book concept and I am grateful for his encouragement.

### Chapter 1

# Wind, Breath and the Holy Spirit

Having a background in science, I often read the Bible thinking of how the authors' view of the world influenced their explanations.  In all cases, I believe, the authors used the most current understanding of the world around them to explain and understand man's relationship with God. If this is so, if we think of what the authors were thinking about the world around us, it will enhance our understanding and appreciation of God.

We can find many examples of science influencing the teachings about God in the Bible  The example that I use is this chapter is wind and breath.

**Wind**

We often only think about wind when it is very windy. We understand why wind occurs: the atmosphere contains molecules that move in response to heat and the rotation of the earth. Hence, wind arises. But for the ancient people this was not clear. They would not have known that air is composed of gases. They would have also needed the knowledge that the earth is a sphere, as this fact is critical to understand how wind arises. They would have needed to know that the equator is warmer than the poles, due to the fact that the sun's rays being more direct at the equator. They would have needed to know that warm air is less dense than cold air, and hence warm air rises.

The knowledge that the earth is a sphere has been known for a long time. The Greeks observed that the moon is round, and they extrapolated that the earth is round. Eratosthenes around 200 BCE did one of the classiest experiment in science ever. He measured the length of a shadow at two places along a meridian at noon on the summer solstice, and calculated the diameter of the earth based upon the length of the shadow using trigonometry. His value is only about 2 per cent from the value now known. The calculation by contemporaries of Columbus, when he sailed in 1492 AD, was less accurate. It was about 25% off. A new piece of information emerged at Columbus's time, though. The earth is not rigorously a sphere; it is an oblate. Centrifugal force due to the rotation of the earth flattens it at the poles and makes it wider at the equator.

Although the knowledge that the earth was round, it does not mean that this information was widely familiar to people during ancient times  The Mesopotamian world origin story assumes that the earth is flat. Even Greek mythology seems to think so. The Greeks named winds according to the wind's direction, and each wind had attributes to it. The west wind, for example, was called *Zephyrus* (Gk. Ζέφυρος [*Zéphyros*]). The gentlest of winds, Zephyrus is known as the messenger of spring. Where was Zephyrus when the west wind was not blowing? If the earth were flat, this is a problem. It was thought that Zephyrus lived in a cave in Thrace.  The word Zephyr is still in our lexicon. The Amtrak train that runs between Chicago and San Francisco is called the Zephyr, denoting that it runs westerly "like the wind."

The writers of the Bible also assumed that the earth was flat. Psalm 103 states:

> [12] *as far as the east is from the west*
>
> *so far has he removed our transgressions from us.*

On a sphere there is no east and west. If you start traveling either east or west in a straight path, you will end up where you started.

In Acts 1:8, the disciples are called to witness to the ends of the earth.

*⁸ But you will receive power when the Holy Spirit comes on you; and you will be my witnesses in Jerusalem, and in all Judea and Samaria, and to the ends of the earth."*

Acts was written about 1000 years after Psalms. A spherical earth does not have an end. A flat earth would have an end with an edge.

Wind can seem very personal. In many parts of the world, winds occur at certain times and these winds are named. Thus, mistral wind occurs in southern France in winter; Santa Ana winds blow from the mountains in Southern California and in Israel, dry, hot winds from Sahara are called Simoon winds. Usually, these winds occur in Spring and Fall, for about 50 days a year. They are also called "Khamsin" meaning 50 in Arabic. Here in Colorado we experience Chinook winds coming from the mountains. Along the east coast of United States "nor-easterners" come up the coast, especially in the winter. "Hurricanes" and "typhoons" are massive storms that affect large areas of the earth surface.

## Wind in the deliverance of Israelites from Egypt

Wind played a role in the deliverance of the Israelite slaves from Egypt. Plagues were sent to Egypt in an attempt to coerce Pharaoh to allow the Israelites to leave. One of these was the Plague of Locusts. Locusts are a type of grasshopper, and, unlike the grasshoppers found here in Colorado, locusts have the ability to swarm (although swarms of grasshoppers are observed in Utah and Nevada). In Exodus 10, the Lord made an east wind blow over the land for a day and a night, and the land became over-run with Locust. Pharaoh capitulated and told Moses that his people could leave. Moses prayed to the Lord, and God made the wind change to the west, and the strong west wind blew the locusts away, and they perished in the Red Sea. Pharaoh reneged on his promise, however.

Wind ultimately was a determining factor in the Israelites' escape from Pharaoh. While they were leaving Egypt, Pharaoh's army pursued them. They were prevented from going east by the Red Sea, so they were potentially trapped. Exodus tells what happened then:

*[21] Then Moses stretched out his hand over the sea, and all that night the Lord drove the sea back with a strong east wind and turned it into dry land. The waters were*

*divided, [22] and the Israelites went through the sea on dry ground, with a wall of water on their right and on their left.*

Following the safe transport over dry land, the seas came together again, and the army and chariots of Pharaoh were drowned by the waters.

**God creates and controls the wind**

The power of God manifested in wind is poetically described in Amos 4:13:

*For behold, He who forms mountains and **creates the wind***

*And declares to man what are His thoughts,*

*He who makes dawn into darkness*

*And treads on the high places of the earth,*

*The Lord God of hosts is His name.*

We all have observed that wind makes leaves rustle and trees bend. From within the house, you may not feel the wind but you can observe it from afar through the window. When the wind speed gets higher, there is howling, and you become worried that the roof may come off.

Wind is very powerful, we do not see it, but we know of its existence through its action.

In John 3, a Pharisee and a member of the ruling class, comes to ask Jesus about what it means to be born again. Jesus uses the capriciousness of wind, not knowing what direction it blows, to describe the Holy Spirt:

> " ⁸ *The wind blows wherever it pleases. You hear its sound, but you cannot tell where it comes from or where it is going. So it is with everyone born of the Spirit.*" **The wind blows where it wishes**, *and you hear its sound, but you do not know where it comes from or where it goes. So it is with everyone who is born of the Spirit.*"

The scriptures emphasize that we cannot know when and where wind comes. But God has power over wind. This power was dramatically illustrated to the disciples as described in Mark 4:35-41. In this passage, Jesus and the disciples are in a boat on the Sea of Galilee:

> ³⁷ *A* **furious squall** *came up, and the waves broke over the boat, so that it was nearly swamped.* ³⁸ *Jesus was in the stern, sleeping on a cushion. The disciples woke him and said to him, "Teacher, don't you care if we drown?"*

*[39]He got up, rebuked the wind and said to the waves, "Quiet! Be still!" Then the **wind** died down and it was completely calm.[40]He said to his disciples, "Why are you so afraid? Do you still have no faith?" [41]They were terrified and asked each other, "Who is this? **Even the wind and the waves obey him!**"*

Jesus is using a known subject of inquiry and awe — how wind arises — to teach the disciples about the Holy Spirit. He is making the Spirit relevant to them using a phenomenon that they experienced and which was wondrous and sometimes terrifying to them.

### Breath

Blow at your hands. You can feel the wind produced by your breath. Both wind and breath arise from the movement of air molecules. As they are the same thing, the sensation you feel from blowing on your hand is the same as you feel from wind. Both wind and breath are used as symbols of the Holy Spirit.

Breath is recognized as essential from the beginning of time. In Genesis 2:7:

*Then the LORD God formed a man from the dust of the ground and breathed into his nostrils the **breath** of life, and the man became a living being.*

What is a difference between us and, say, a rock? Both are made by God, but we have breath.

For ages, the act of breathing signified life. At the Kennedy grave site in Arlington, two Kennedy babies are buried. One is named "Patrick", a baby who died two days after birth. The second is labeled "Daughter". She was not named on the cemetery stone, as she was still-born and never breathed air. Breathing meant life, and for ages breath signified that the baby was now human with a soul.

The symbolism of breath and wind is pervasive throughout the scriptures. In Hebrew a single word ruach ( רוּחַ) translates as breath, wind, and spirit. Greek, the language of the New Testament, has separate words used to translate ruach. The Greek words are as follows:

>**Breath** is: αναπνοή anapnoí;
>
>**Spirit** is: πνεύμα pnéuma;
>
>**Wind** is άνεμος ánemos.

All three Greek words have made it into the English lexicon. The Greek word for lung is: πνεύμονας pnéumonas. The lung disease pneumonia originates from this Greek word.

Apnea, the condition of temporarily stopping breathing, comes from the Greek word for breath. Anemone, in the buttercup family, have small flowers that open in wind. The flower's name comes from the Greek word for wind.

When we read the Old Testament we are reading an <u>English</u> translation of a <u>Greek</u> translation of <u>Hebrew</u>. The translation of Hebrew to Greek resulted as a result of world events. The Greek general Alexander the Great conquered Palestine and Egypt in 332 BC, and by 323 BC, the time of his death he had conquered most of the known world. This conquest dispersed Greek culture to all the conquered countries. After his death, his empire was split into two. Palestine area was lumped together with Eqypt under Ptolemy. The Greeks were interested in introducing Greek culture to people under their rule. Ptolemy Philadelphus (285-246 BC), king of the western segment of the Greek empire that had Egypt as its center, initiated translation of the Hebrew texts. The first five books of the Bible were translated from Hebrew to Greek, followed by other texts. The translation was made by a committee of 70 people. It was made with care and scholarship.

In each case of its use, the committee would have had to decide how to translate ruach. The word is translated to breath in Job 27:3:

*"as long as I have life within me, the **breath** of God in my nostrils, my lips will not say anything wicked and my tongue will not utter lies."*

The powerfulness of breath can be seen in the vision of Ezekiel 37. The prophet in his dream sees a valley covered with dry bones. These bones represent the Jews who were in exile and had given up hope.

*⁴Then he said to me, "Prophesy to these bones and say to them, '**Dry bones**, hear the word of the Lord! ⁵ This is what the Sovereign Lord says to these bones: I will make **breath enter you, and you will come to life.** ⁶ I will attach tendons to you and make flesh come upon you and cover you with skin; I will put breath in you, and you will come to life. Then you will know that I am the Lord.'"....*

*⁹Then he said to me, "Prophesy to the breath; prophesy, son of man, and say to it, 'This is what the Sovereign Lord says: **Come, breath, from the four winds and breathe into these slain, that they may live.**'" ¹⁰So I prophesied as he commanded me, and breath entered them; they came to life and stood up on their feet—a vast army.*

Ezekiel lived during the time of exile in Babylon. The interpretation of the vision is that the dry bones represent the Israelites in Babylon. Even if they have lost their homeland and are "dry bones", meaning they have lost hope and faith, God's breath is able to restore their faith. The passage also shows how wind and breath were associated.

Luke writes in Acts 17 that God gives us breath and life:

[24] *"The God who made the world and everything in it is the Lord of heaven and earth and does not live in temples built by human hands. [25] And he is not served by human hands, as if he needed anything. Rather, he himself gives everyone **life** and **breath** and everything else.*

### Pentecost and the Holy Spirit

The Christian faith has a tenet of a Triune God. That is to say, there is one God, but He manifests in three parts: the Father, the Son and the Holy Spirit. God the Son, is easy to conceptualize; He is Jesus whose birth we celebrate at Christmas and death and resurrection at Easter. God the Father, the Creator is also understandable (somewhat). God the Holy Spirit is  a harder concept.

A description of Pentecost, the Christian celebration of the appearance of the Holy Spirit is given in Acts 2:2:

*...they were all together in one place. Suddenly a sound like the **blowing of a violent wind** came from heaven and filled the whole house where they were sitting...*

The disciples would have known the significance of wind because there was a long history of using wind to describe the Holy Spirit.

**Breath in our worship**

The scripture in Psalm 150:6 states:

*"Let everything that has breath praise the Lord! Praise the Lord."*

This passage is exuberant expression that everything that is living can praise the Lord.

The psalms were songs — they were originally sung. In singing, one needs breath control. The melodies of the psalms are forgotten, but some people recommend reading the Psalms using breath regulation. For instance the first line of Psalm 23 reads:

*"The Lord is my Shepherd, I shall not want"*

Try reading the first phrase breathing in, as you allow the Lord to come in, and read the second phrase breathing out, as you let go of the cares of life.

The hymn "Breathe on me Breath of God" was written by Edwin Hatch in 1878. It is a favorite in our church. Here are the lyrics of two verses:

Breathe on me, Breath of God,

fill me with life anew,

that I may love the way you love,

and do what you would do.


Breathe on me, **Breath** of God,

Till I am wholly Thine,

Until this earthly part of me

Glows with Thy **fire** divine.


Wind is a symbol of the Holy Spirit. A second symbol of the Holy Spirit is fire, which is discussed in Chapter 2. The second verse of the hymn quoted above combines both symbols of breath and fire.

The hymn "Breathe on me Breath of God" is usually sung slowly and sweetly during the middle of the service while we are contemplative. But I think that it should be sung loud and with the beat marked by drums at the end of the service as we rambunctiously leave! It is written in 3/4 time. Sing it like a dance, as you waltz out of church and into the world!

Remember even if you are "dry bones' without faith and hope as described in Ezekiel 37, the Holy Spirit can breathe life into you. So, instead of waltzing, perhaps you should raucously sashay out of church into the world singing "Dry Bones:"

Them bones, them bones gonna walk around

Them bones, them bones gonna walk around

Them bones, them bones gonna walk around

I hear the word of the Lord!

### Chapter 2

# Fire and the Holy Spirit

Christianity has the tenet that God is expressed in three persons: Father, Son and Holy Ghost. Pentecost is celebrated on the fiftieth day after Easter for the gift of the Holy Spirit to the disciples and believers after Jesus's resurrection.

The day of Pentecost is described in Acts 2:

*When the day of Pentecost came, they were all together in one place. Suddenly a sound like the **blowing of a violent wind** came from heaven and filled the whole house where they were sitting. They saw what seemed to be **tongues of fire** that separated and came to rest on each of them. All of them were filled with the Holy Spirit and began to speak in other tongues as the Spirit enabled them.*

There are thus two symbols of the Holy Spirit — wind and fire. We discussed wind in the previous chapter. Of the two symbols for Pentecost, fire is better known. Our church has a tradition of wearing red on Pentecostal Sunday, to memorialize the fire of the Holy Spirit. In this chapter we are going examine how fire became a symbol for the Israelites and for Christians.

**Fire in science**

The chemical equation for fire that burns items that were alive (trees, grass, coal, oil, etc) is:

$$[C, H] + O_2 \longrightarrow CO_2 + H_2O + \text{energy (heat and light)}$$
(Equation 1)

The brackets indicate that carbon [C] and [H] containing molecules react with oxygen, $O_2$, to form carbon dioxide, $CO_2$, and water, $H_2O$.

Food that we eat consists of carbon containing molecules, [C]. The chemical equation that described the metabolism of food (bread, meat, candy bar, Brussels sprouts, etc) to give us energy is:

$$[C, H] + O_2 \longrightarrow CO_2 + H_2O + \text{energy (heat and light)}$$
(Equation 2)

Hey... equation 1 and 2 are identical! Yes, both chemical reactions start with a carbon compound that reacts with oxygen. They both end with formation of carbon dioxide and water. Carbon dioxide is a gas, and water is liquid and gas. When you lose weight by dieting, your extra pounds escape to the atmosphere as $CO_2$ and water. This is the same for fire — the log that is burning in the fireplace loses weight and becomes gas.

But the mechanisms are quite different for burning carbon containing compounds and metabolizing carbon-containing food in our body.

In metabolism, the reaction between food and carbon dioxide takes a series of steps. The reaction of each step is catalyzed by an enzyme. A catalyst is a substance that makes a chemical reaction go faster. An enzyme is the name for a catalyst in the body. All enzymes are proteins. I counted that there are 24 enzymes in our body that are required to change one sugar molecule into $CO_2$ and $H_2O$, as in equation 2. The steps for food metabolism is carried out in a regulated way. As you are reading this you are probably not thinking about your big toe. It is doing nothing, and it is also not using food to get energy. But, if you wiggle your toe, suddenly fat and carbohydrate that is stored in your body is mobilized, and it is used to give energy to the muscles moving your toe. Blood flows to your toe, carrying oxygen. Your toe is now making carbon dioxide and water.  Some heat is produced. You notice that you get warmer when you exercise and you know to wiggle your toes when you are outside in very cold weather.

Fire has the same chemical products as metabolism, but it is unregulated. It occurs by what is known as a free radical reaction. In most compounds, there are pairs of electrons.  Two atoms are held together by two electrons. In free-radical compounds, one electron does not have a partner. This "free" electron of the molecule makes the molecule unstable and reactive with pretty much everything else.  When it reacts with another molecule another free radical is produced, and so on. Suddenly, you have a gigantic chemical reaction with much heat being produced.  The reaction continues until the fuel source is depleted or until oxygen is no longer being supplied.

Without the initiation of the chemical reaction, things that burn are generally stable. Red wood trees in California are 2000 years old. The Horyu-ji temple in Japan is a wooden structure that is over 1600 years old.  It was shocking to see newscasts of the fire of Notre Dame Cathedral in Paris, in April, 2019. The corner stone of this Cathedral was laid in 1163 AD and the oak beams holding the roof were stable until a spark started them on fire. We had a large fire here in Colorado at the end of 2021. Over 1000 homes burnt. In these homes, families safely raised their children, until a spark ignited the fire and the homes and contents were completely destroyed.

Fire is probably the most dramatic chemical reaction that we routinely observe. Fire is essential for life as we currently live, but it is also dangerous. It can be regulated by limiting fuel; this method is used when a candle burns or when you use a gas stove. It can be put out by limiting oxygen supply; this method is the basis of foam used in airport for plane fires. Smothering fire is also sometimes the basis of putting out forest fires. Substances that char the surface of combustible surfaces are sometimes used to prevent oxygen to get to the substance. Fire can also be slowed by supplying "quenchers". These are chemical compounds react with the free radicals produced by the fire chemistry, and prevent or slow the formation of further free radicals. The kind of molecules that quench fire are added to children's pajamas to make them fire resistant, for instance. Chemical reactions go slower as temperature decreases (because molecules need to collide to react and molecules move faster at high temperatures). So cooling a fire, with water or another means, will help to put out the fire.

**Ancient view of fire**

When humans were able to control fire is unknown, but archeological evidence indicates that fire was used for a long time, perhaps 300,000 years, perhaps longer. Fire is used to cook food, clear land of vegetation, scare away dangerous animals, make pottery and for light. It is used for social reasons too. We, today, still like to gather around a camp fire — it represents warmth and camaraderie.

The historian Felipe Fernandez-Armesto records that ancient peoples traded fire. Even if these people knew how to start a fire, they had the belief that someone else's fire was perhaps better, and therefore they would trade embers. The importance of fire remains in many religions. A central feature of the Zorastrian religion — a contemporary religion to Judaism and also extant in the Middle East — is that fire purifies.

Fire is a purifier but it is also destructive. Both aspects are recognized in the Bible. (The next chapter will describe fire as punishment.)

**Fire in the Bible: Light and direction.**

Moses is a great hero in the Bible. He led the Israelites from slavery in Egypt to the promised land. In Exodus 3:2, God speaks to him from a burning bush, instructing him to be his people's leader.

*Now Moses was tending the flock of Jethro his father-in-law, the priest of Midian, and he led the flock to the far side of the wilderness and came to Horeb, the mountain of God ²There the angel of the Lord appeared to him in flames of **fire from within a bush**. Moses saw that though the bush was on fire it did not burn up.*

Fire in Exodus was a symbol of deliverance. As Moses leads the Israelites through the desert, Exodus 13:21-22 describes that they are led by a pillar of fire:

*By day the LORD went ahead **of** them in a pillar of cloud to guide them on their way and by night in a **pillar of fire** to give them light, so that they could travel by day or night. ²² Neither the pillar of cloud by day nor the **pillar of fire** by night left its place in front **of** the people.*

**Fire in worship**

Fire was commanded to be part of the ritual of the religion of the Israelites in Exodus 27:20-21:

*Command the children of Israel that they bring thee the purest oil of the olives, and beaten with a pestle: **that a lamp may burn always,** in the tabernacle of the testimony, without the veil that hangs before the testimony.*

This is reiterated in Leviticus 6:12:

*The **fire** on the altar shall be kept burning on it; it shall not go out. The priest shall burn wood on it every morning, and he shall arrange the burnt offering on it and shall burn on it the fat of the peace offerings.*

The Jewish celebration of Hanukkah harkens back to this custom of having oil burning in the Temple. During the rededication of the second temple, about 600 BCE, it was discovered that the consecrated oil was lacking. But, miraculously, the small amount of oil available. This oil would normally have lasted one day but it lasted seven days. During Hanukkah, candles in a menorah are lit. A menorah is a candelabrum with eight branches and a central socket.

In Roman Catholic churches, a lamp is kept lit in the chancel to symbolize that the Holy Spirit is present.

### Fire as purification for metals

Metals are needed for weapons, cookware, tools, chariots. Copper and gold occur in the earth as pure elements, i.e., not combined with other elements. Copper was probably the first metal used, and archeological evidence indicates that it was used as early as 7500 BC. Copper is more abundant than gold, but gold has been held valuable from ancient times to now because it does not tarnish.

During the time between Abraham and the end of the Bible, people learned to purify metals and to make ever stronger metals. To purify a metal you must start with an ore rich in that metal. In Job 28:1-2:

> *There is a mine for silver and a place where gold is refined. Iron is taken from the earth, and copper is smelted from ore.*

Melting point of metals is the basis of purification. Pure metals have different melting points. To purify gold, for instance, you start with an ore rich in gold. When you heat it to 1064 C (1948 F), the gold melts, and you can pour the liquid gold out, leaving the solid material containing other metals. Or you can scoop the un-melted ore floating on top of the liquid gold. In either way, impurities are removed, and purified gold is obtained.

Metals have different metal points and by changing the heat that the ore is subjected to, different metals can be extracted. Melting points are: silver: 961 C (1761 F); gold: 1064 C (1948 F:; copper 1034 C (1983 F), tin 232 C (449 F).

Ancient people were able to craft very beautiful objects from metal. A gold wreath excavated from Ur, the home area of Abraham is at the University of Pennsylvania Museum. This wreath was found in the grave of Queen Puabi, a queen in the Mesopotamia at around 2600 BC. When Abraham lived is not exactly known, but Puabi likely was either a contemporary or predated him.

Gold was a thing of value and indicated wealth. Genesis 13 records that Abraham was wealthy:

> *So Abram went up from Egypt to the Negev, with his wife and everything he had, and Lot went with him. ² Abram had become very wealthy in livestock and in **silver** and **gold**.*

The value of gold was recognized by Moses (dates unknown but probably 1500 - 1300 BCE). In Exodus 3:21-22 Moses instructs the Israelites to take gold, silver and clothing:

*...and when you go, you shall not go empty,* [22] *but each woman shall ask of her neighbor, and any woman who lives in her house, for **silver** and **gold** jewelry, and for clothing. You shall put them on your sons and on your daughters. So you shall plunder the Egyptians."*

You probably remember that this gold did not end with a good result. The Israelites disobeyed the commandment from God not to serve other gods and they made it into a Golden Calf, as told in Exodus 32.

Ability to purify metals advanced as people learned methods to build hotter fires, allowing for metals with higher melting points to be purified. Charcoal burns hotter than wood. Charcoal is made from wood by heating in the absence of air; water and volatile substances vaporize leaving charcoal. If you like to grill food, you know that charcoal is preferred over wood because charcoal produces a hotter fire. In the same way, coal is heated to make coke. Coke is used now the fuel used in steel industry.

Another advance in producing metals was to blow air through the molten rock. Impurities would oxidize and form a scum, called dross, on top. Dross was thrown out.

The prophet Ezekiel, who lived in Babylon in the 6th century BC, used the analogy of dross to the Israelites, when he prophesied the destruction of Jerusalem in Ezekiel 22:

*17 Then the word of the Lord came to me: 18 "Son of man, the people of Israel have become **dross** to me; all of them are the copper, tin, iron and lead left inside a furnace. They are but the dross of silver. 19 Therefore this is what the Sovereign Lord says: 'Because you have all become dross, I will gather you into Jerusalem. 20 As silver, copper, iron, lead and tin are gathered into a furnace to be melted with a fiery blast, so will I gather you in my anger and my wrath and put you inside the city and melt you. 21 I will gather you and I will blow on you with my fiery wrath, and you will be melted inside her. 22 As silver is melted in a furnace, so you will be melted inside her, and you will know that I the Lord have poured out my wrath on you.'*

A list of metals used by the Israelites is given in Numbers 31:

*21 Then Eleazar the priest said to the soldiers who had gone into battle, "This is what is required by the law that the Lord gave Moses: 22 **Gold, silver, bronze, iron, tin,***

***lead** [23] and anything else that can withstand fire must be put through the fire, and then it will be clean.*

### Fire as purification in religious beliefs

The Israelites, like all people, used things they were familiar with, to explain their religious beliefs. It is no stretch then, that they would use refining metals as an analogy for God purifying mankind.

In Zechariah 13 the prophet is telling of the need for repentance and purification, Verses 8-9 makes the analogy to metal purification:

> *[8]In the whole land," declares the Lord, "two-thirds will be struck down and perish; yet one-third will be left in it [9] This third I will put into the **fire**; I will **refine them like silver** and **test them like gold.** They will call on my name and I will answer them; I will say, 'They are my people,' and they will say, 'The Lord is our God.'"*

Malachi 3:2-3 records a similar sentiment:

> *[2]But who can endure the day of his coming, and who can stand when he appears? For he is like a refiner's fire and like fullers' soap. [3]He will sit as a refiner and purifier of silver, and he will **purify** the sons of Levi and **refine them***

*like gold and silver, and they will bring offerings in righteousness to the Lord.*

Fire remains a central symbol in Israelite scripture. Psalm 66:10 summarizes:

*For you, O God, have tested us; you have tried us as silver is tried.*

## Holy Spirit visualized

When you look at a fire you can think about how fire is used as a symbol of the Holy Spirit. Fire is beautiful, useful and somewhat mysterious.

I greatly enjoyed visiting Israel 20 ago. I was amazed how my perception of Israel was influenced by art I had seen. I somehow pictured that Israel would look like a medieval European village as in the art I had seen— and it is not like that.

Undoubtedly, like my preconception of Israel, our image of the Holy Spirit is influenced by artists who tried to depict Pentecost. In this chapter, we discussed the symbolism of fire in the Bible. Fire is an intriguing object for artists to illustrate. It involves light and it is constantly moving. It is no wonder that fire has been used by artists throughout the ages to represent the Holy Spirit.

I refer you to some pictures. An interesting etching can be found by googling "Hirschvogel pentecost". The etching was made by Augustin Hirschvogel  and the full title is "Pentecost, from Old and New Testaments" by Augustin Hirschvogel, 1548 (Metropolitan Museum of Art). The artist depicts the fire on the disciples' heads as described In Acts 2:3: "And divided tongues as of fire appeared to them and rested on each one of them." The disciples are kneeling and they hold their arms out in wonderment and acceptance.

A modern painting of Pentecost can be seen by googling "Jennifer Allison Pentecost". This painting was downloaded to web on August 2018. The artist attempts to show the movement of fire, and thereby she conveys both wind and fire, the two symbols of the Holy Spirit. The picture is exuberant in its use of color. Some of the disciples appear to raise their arms in ecstasy whereas others hold their hands together, as in prayer. They are all kneeling. This painting is available printed on a colorful tote bag.

**Chapter 3**

# Downsides of Wind and Fire

### Wind

Wind and fire as symbols of the Holy Spirit are discussed in the previous chapters. Wind and fire are integral to life and they are comforting when not in excess. But, they have down sides. Both Old and New Testaments have exciting stories about wind when sailing. Jonah was commanded to preach to Ninevah. But Jonah disobeyed and sailed in the opposite direction. But, a big storm came up, as related in Jonah 1.

> *⁴Then the Lord sent a **great wind** on the sea, and such a violent storm arose that the ship threatened to break up. ⁵All the sailors were afraid and each cried out to his own god. And they threw the cargo into the sea to lighten the ship.*

*But Jonah had gone below deck, where he lay down and fell into a deep sleep. ⁶The captain went to him and said, "How can you sleep? Get up and call on your god! Maybe he will take notice of us so that we will not perish."....*

*¹¹ The **sea was getting rougher and rougher**. So they asked him [Jonah], "What should we do to you to make the sea calm down for us?"*

*¹² "Pick me up and throw me into the sea," he replied, "and it will become calm. I know that it is my fault that this great storm has come upon you."*

*¹³ Instead, the men did their best to row back to land. But they could not, for the **sea grew even wilder** than before. ¹⁴ Then they cried out to the Lord, "Please, Lord, do not let us die for taking this man's life. Do not hold us accountable for killing an innocent man, for you, Lord, have done as you pleased." ¹⁵ Then they took Jonah and threw him overboard, and the **raging sea grew calm**.*

In the New Testament the adventures of Paul certainly rival those of Indiana Jones. Paul records that he was wrecked three times (2 Corinthians 11:25). The events when he was sailing to Rome are given Acts 27:

*[13] When a gentle south wind began to blow, they saw their opportunity; so they weighed anchor and sailed along the shore of Crete. [14] Before very long, a **wind of hurricane force**, called the Northeaster, swept down from the island. [15] The ship was caught by the storm and could not head into the wind; so we gave way to it and were driven along.*

The storm that Paul endured was certainly a very big one — lasting 14 days with wind and darkness. Under cloud cover, the sailors would not have been able to tell directions from the stars. So, in addition to be suffering danger from high waves, they would not have known where they were,.

The people in the Bible knew the power of storm. Excessive wind became a symbol of futility and punishment.

### Wind as futility

Features of wind are that it comes and goes, and, while you know that it exists, you cannot catch it. These properties make it a suitable symbol of futility. This is eloquently seen in writings attributed to a Son of David, perhaps Solomon, in Ecclesiastes. The author uses wind as one example of meaninglessness In Ecclesiastes 1:

*² "Meaningless! Meaningless!" says the Teacher. "Utterly meaningless! Everything is meaningless."*

*³ What do people gain from all their labors at which they toil under the sun?*

*⁴ Generations come and generations go, but the earth remains forever.*

*⁵ The sun rises and the sun sets, and hurries back to where it rises.*

*⁶ **The wind blows to the south and turns to the north; …***

*⁸ All things are wearisome more than one can say…*

Solomon was a magnificent king, but he recognizes that all of his accomplishments are insignificant by saying that they were chasing after the wind. In Ecclesiastes 2:

*¹¹ Yet when I surveyed all that my hands had done and what I had toiled to achieve, everything was meaningless, **a chasing after the wind;** nothing was gained under the sun.*

We often evaluate our accomplishments by comparing them to what other people accomplish. This leads to envy. Everyone must eventually recognize that no matter how rich you are, how smart you are, how good looking you are, there is someone richer, or smarter, or better looking than you. Ecclesiastes 4 states that work to achieve more fame than someone else is futile:

*⁴And I saw that all toil and all achievement spring from one person's envy of another. This too is meaningless, **a chasing after the wind**.*

That wind has no value is used in Proverbs 11 to express that whoever brings disaster to family will inherit nothing:

*²⁹Whoever brings ruin on their family will **inherit only wind**, and the fool will be servant to the wise.*

### Wind as doubt

In the New Testament, both Paul and James use wind to illustrate doubtfulness of faith. In Ephesians 4 he warns of doubt brought about by people who scheme to sow doubt:

*¹⁴Then we will no longer be infants, tossed back and forth by the waves, and **blown here and there by every wind of teaching** and by the cunning and craftiness of people in their deceitful scheming. ¹⁵Instead, speaking the truth in love, we will grow to become in every respect the mature body of him who is the head, that is, Christ.*

James (in James 1) uses similar language. This passage is evocative because, just as waves have no control over wind, so a doubter goes from thing to thing, without direction:

*⁵If any of you lacks wisdom, you should ask God, who gives generously to all without finding fault, and it will be given to you. ⁶ But when you ask, you must believe and not doubt, because the one who doubts is like a wave of the sea, **blown and tossed by the wind.***

## Wind as punishment

Wind can be destructive and deadly. Wind is used as a destructive force in God's judgement.

Israel, to this day, experiences drying winds that come from the Sahara desert. Hosea, in chapter 13, talks about death and the punishment of Israel for being disobedient. The power of wind is described:

*¹⁴ "I will deliver this people from the power of the grave;   I will redeem them from deat. Where, O death, are your plague? ,Where, O grave, is your destruction?*
*"I will have no compassion,*
*¹⁵ even though he thrives among his brothers. **An east wind from the Lord will come,   blowing in from the desert;** his spring will fail   and his well dry up. His storehouse will be plundered   of all its treasures.*

Isaiah, the prophet, foresees the destruction of Ephraim due to wickedness. Ephraim was one of the sons of Joseph, and one of the twelve tribes. It also can refer to the Northern Kingdom, Israel. Here is a passage from Isaiah 28:

*² See, the Lord has one who is powerful and strong. Like a hailstorm and a **destructive wind**, like a driving rain and a flooding downpour,  he will throw it forcefully to the ground.*

In Jeremiah 30, the Lord promises Judah and Israel that their enemies will be punished:

*²³ See, the storm of the Lord will burst out in wrath, a **driving wind swirling down,**  on the heads of the wicked.*

In the New Testament, wind symbolizes adversity in Jesus' promise that wind will not prevail against a house (a life) built on a solid foundation (Matt 7:27).

*²⁴ "Therefore everyone who hears these words of mine and puts them into practice is like a wise man who built his house on the rock. ²⁵ The rain came down, the streams rose, and the **winds** blew and beat against that house; yet it did not fall, because it had its foundation on the rock. ²⁶ But everyone who hears these words of mine and does not put them into practice is like a foolish man who built his house on sand. ²⁷ The rain came down, the streams rose, and the*

*winds blew and beat against that house, and it fell with a*
*great crash."*

## Fire as judgment and punishment

Refining of metals was described in Chapter 2. The refining method is a separation method — what is desirable is separated from the slag, which is thrown out. The undesirable is rejected. We can look at refining as either obtaining pure substance, or we can look at it as throwing out the impure.

Old Testament the punishment of God by fire is terrifying and immediate as seen Numbers 11:1. This incident occurred when the Israelites complained when Moses was leading them out of Egypt to the Promised Land:

*And the people complained in the hearing of the Lord*
*about their misfortunes, and when the Lord heard it, his*
*anger was kindled, and the **fire of the Lord burned** among*
*them and consumed some outlying parts of the camp.*

And God's response was powerful as in 2 Kings 1:9-12 when the king threatened Elijah with a captain with fifty men:

*But Elijah answered the captain of fifty, "If I am a man*
*of God, let fire come down from heaven and consume you*

*and your fifty." Then **fire came down from heaven and
consumed him and his fifty**. Again the king sent to him
another captain of fifty men with his fifty. And he
answered and said to him, "O man of God, this is the
king's order, 'Come down quickly!'" But Elijah answered
them, "If I am a man of God, let fire come down from
heaven and consume you and your fifty." Then the **fire of
God** came down from heaven and consumed him and his
fifty.*

On the other hand, Isaiah 43:2 for those that follow the
Lord:

*When you pass through the waters, I will be with you; and
through the rivers, they shall not overwhelm you; when
**you walk through fire you shall not be burned,** and the
flame shall not consume you.*

### New Testament

The theme of fire, refining, judgement and punishment
seen in the Old Testament is further developed in the New
Testament. In fact, it seems to me, the view of Hell and
Damnation becomes more defined than in the New Testament.

There is a definite day of judgement. For instance, in Matthew 25:41

> *"Then he will say to those on his left, 'Depart from me, you cursed, into the **eternal fire** prepared for the devil and his angels.*

In 1 Peter 1:7, the apostle Peter writes of the ultimate purpose of purification:

> *So that the tested genuineness of your faith—more precious than gold that perishes though it is tested by fire—may be found to result in praise and glory and honor at the revelation of Jesus Christ.*

John the Baptist realizes the purification of fire in Matthew 3:11:

> *"I baptize you with water for repentance, but he who is coming after me is mightier than I, whose sandals I am not worthy to carry. He will baptize you with the **Holy Spirit and fire.***

### Brimstone in judgement

Most fire that we observe is the reaction of a carbon containing molecule with molecular oxygen. Charcoal and coke, used in refining, are made of carbon. But oxygen will react with many of the elements. One notable case is the reaction with sulfur. In some parts of the world sulfur exists in pure form, called brimstone. (Carbon can also exist in pure form, as graphite and diamonds, and these things can also burn).

The reaction of sulfur with $O_2$ is:

$$S + O_2 \longrightarrow SO_2 + \text{ energy (heat and light)}$$

(Equation 1)

When sulfur is a component of a living thing, it is chemically combined with hydrogen plus other elements, and the reaction is:

$$[SH] + O_2 \longrightarrow SO_2 + H_2O + \text{ energy (heat and light)}$$

(Equation 2)

In the case of Equations 1 and 2, the reaction of oxygen with either the element sulfur or sulfur in a compound, produces $SO_2$, sulfur dioxide. When carbon burns it forms carbon dioxide. $CO_2$. Carbon dioxide dissolves in water and forms carbonic acid. This is what is found in carbonated water, and it gives a tang to water. It is mildly acidic, but not dangerous. $SO_2$ also dissolves in water, but dissolved in water it forms sulfuric acid. Sulfuric acid is a strong acid, and it is dangerous. It can burn skin, make holes in clothes, permanently damage lungs, blind you, and even dissolve many kinds of rocks.

In addition to being dangerous, many sulfur compounds are smelly. Both hair and feathers contain protein molecules that contain sulfur. These sulfur containing compounds account for the obnoxious smell when hair or feathers are burned. A sulfur compound is responsible for the smell of rotten eggs. The yolk of eggs contain a relatively high amount of sulfur-containing amino acids, which are used to make feathers on the chick. Sulfur is also found in coal and crude oil, substances originally coming from living things. Many rocks contain sulfur. Pyrite, a beautiful mirrored rock, is made of iron and sulfur. Because sulfur is so prevalent in substances that we use industrially, $SO_2$ is a dangerous side product of many industrial processes.

**Sulfur in the body**

We are painting sulfur as a villain. But, sulfur is a requirement for life too. Three of the body's amino acids contain sulfur. These amino acids are essential for the proteins in our body to function properly. Vitamins biotin and thiamine contain sulfur. Bonds between S groups (called S-S bonds) are what makes hair curly and which are modified when a permanent is used to make straight hair curly.

Sulfur is required for the growth of all known living things, including plants. Sulfur is used as a fertilizer in agriculture, in places where soil lacks sulfur.

**Brimstone in history**

Pure sulfur in the form of brimstone deposits are often found around volcanos, and the area around the Mediterranean Sea has many volcanos. In Greek mythology Homer (about 8th century BCE) recounts the use of sulfur dioxide by Odysseus to fumigate a room in which he had killed his wife's lovers. The beginnings of practical and industrial uses of sulfur are credited to the Egyptians, who reportedly used sulfur dioxide for bleaching cotton as early as 1600 BCE.

The whole Mediterranean area is seismically active. The Dead Sea and the Sea of Galilee lie in the Great Rift, which is where two continental plates are moving away from each other. An earthquake was recorded in Amos 1,1. Earthquakes occurred at the death and resurrection of Jesus Matthew 27:51-54; Matthew 28:2). Another earthquake was described in Acts 16:26:

*and suddenly there came a great earthquake, so that the foundations of the prison house were shaken; and immediately all the doors were opened and everyone's chains were unfastened.*

A very active volcanic region stretches from the bay of Naples in southern Italy to the island of Sicily. In Sicily, brimstone (which is a name for pure sulfur) has been mined for 3000 years.

So Israelites would have had available sulfur. They would have known that the burning of sulfur is even more noxious than the burning of wood, which is made of carbon-based molecules.

In Genesis 19, Sodom and Gomorrah are destroyed with rain of fire and brimstone, suggesting volcanic activity. The Israelites are warned that the same punishment would occur to them should they disobey God's covenant (Deuteronomy 29).

### Sulfur as punishment

In Revelation, the punishment of Hell is worse than ordinary carbon fire, since it is also compounded by sulfur. Here are some passages that describes the punishment:

Revelation 14:10:

*He also will drink the wine of God's wrath, poured full strength into the cup of his anger, and he will be tormented with **fire and sulfur** in the presence of the holy angels and in the presence of the Lamb.*

Revelation 21:8 :

*But as for the cowardly, the faithless, the detestable, as for murderers, the sexually immoral, sorcerers, idolaters, and all liars, their portion will be in the lake that burns with **fire and sulfur**, which is the second death."*

John, the author of Revelation, knew about burning of sulfur. The description of a "lake" in Revelation 21:8 sounds like a volcano caldera. John was a well-traveled person. Perhaps he heard about, or even saw, a caldera.

**Some speculation**

In writing this I do not want to "de-mythologize" the Bible. That is, I do not want to use *a priori* naturalism to explain everything that is described in the Bible. The basis of Faith is just that — faith. I am trying to make the case that the Israelites used their observation of natural phenomena to describe and understand God. But, in this last section I am changing my focus a bit. I am doing the reverse of the main thrust of this book — I am seeing if science can shed light on two particular events in the Bible. This section is called "Some speculation" because it is speculation.

In the previous section, we noted that God gave the Israelites a **pillar of cloud and fire** to direct their travel from Egypt to the Promised Land.

Sulfur is widely found in the Middle East and it has been burned throughout history. My brother (John Vander Kooi) pointed out to me characteristics of burning sulfur. It burns with a pale blue flame. The flame is not visible in bright sunlight; burning sulfur will show smoke but not flame in sunlight. The flame, however, is visible at night.

Now, I want to point out an interesting feature of this pillar. In Exodus 13:21:

> *By day the Lord went ahead **of** them in a **pillar of** cloud to guide them on their way and by night in a **pillar of fire** to give them light, so that they could travel by day or night.*

Therefore, the pillar had characteristics of what people would observe for a sulfur fire - smoke during the day and a flame at night.

Brimstone can start burning from a lightning strike. The pillar of cloud and pillar of fire was used by the Israelites as a guide during their 40 years in the desert before they made it to the promised land. The walking distance from Cairo, Egypt to Jerusalem, Israel is about 760 km, or 475 miles. If you walk 10 miles/ day, it would take about 48 days to go from Egypt to Jerusalem. Allowing for rest on the Sabbath, this would be about 2 months. Since women, children and animals were along on the trek, this time would be extended — but hardly to 40 years (14,610 days). The pillar appears to erratic in its motion. Could that because it was random fires occurring at sulfur deposits?

The Bible recounts another interpretation for the long time in the story: the disobedience of the Israelites while Moses was receiving the Ten Commandments on Mount Sinai. While Moses was away, the people melted gold and made a Golden Calf and worshiped this idol. The wandering of the Israelites for 40 years was punishment by God and this time ensured that anyone who participated in this sin, did not enter the promised land (Numbers 14).

Another speculative example of fire is the story of the burning bush; this story also concerns Moses and is also described in Exodus. It occurred earlier in Moses's life. Moses grew up in Pharaoh's court in Egypt, where he married an Israelite woman.  Exodus 3 recounts how God called Moses to lead his people out of Egypt. God speaks from a burning bush to tell Moses that he should lead his people out of slavery:

> *Now Moses was tending the flock of Jethro his father-in-law, the priest of Midian, and he led the flock to the far side of the wilderness and came to Horeb, the mountain of God.* [2]*There the angel of the Lord appeared to him in* ***flames of fire from within a bush.*** *Moses saw that though the* ***bush was on fire it did not burn up.*** [3]*So Moses thought, "I will go over and see this strange sight—why the bush does not burn up."*
>
> [4]*When the Lord saw that he had gone over to look, God called to him from within the bush, "Moses! Moses!"*
> *And Moses said, "Here I am."*

Why did the bush not burn up? Sulfur ignites at a lower temperature than wood. This is the reason that sulfur is so useful in the head of matches. Presumably, the fire is not as hot either, and perhaps sulfur was burning around the bush without igniting it. This is pure speculation; we can never know for sure. But we could do an experiment to see if under some conditions a sulfur fire would not ignite wood. The experiment that I envision is as follows: first cut two branches from a bush or tree, or use two sticks of wood. Chose branches or sticks that are as near as possible identical to each other. Find a location outside and far away from anything flammable. Start a fire from charcoal in one grill and from brimstone in another grill. (Sulfur is available for purchase on-line from Amazon; it is used as a fertilizer and can also be obtained in Garden stores). Stand up-wind from the two grills; you do not want to breathe the fumes. Put a branch in each fire, and observe whether burning rates of the two branches differ in the two fires. Does the branch in the charcoal grill get ignited sooner and burn faster?

I am not going to do this experiment right now. I live in Colorado in a suburban area. My neighbors will not appreciate $SO_2$ fumes. Fire danger is always high in our dry climate. Besides, this is not a definitive experiment. The rate of burning, and hence temperature, depends upon how fast oxygen is supplied to the fire. This rate will not be exactly controlled how I envision the experiment. Nevertheless, someday I may still try it out of curiosity.

### Chapter 4

# Water and Baptism

### Water is central to life

All known species of life on the earth require water to live. I say "known". Scientist are taught never to say that something is proven. So, this is not to say that there may be some living thing on earth that is water-free. There is some evidence that archaea may live deep in the earth, near where it is so hot the rock is liquid as magma. Perhaps these extremophiles do not require water?

The requirement of water for life on earth is so pervasive, that a criteria for searching for possible extraterrestrial life is the presence of liquid water. No life on earth has been discovered that does not need water.

Water is unique among the substances on the surface of the earth in that it occurs naturally in solid, liquid and gaseous forms. Living things require liquid water, but to have rain and moisture on land, it is necessary for water to evaporate to form gas. Gaseous water is invisible to our eye. But the presence of water in the atmosphere can be surmised by the presence of clouds. Clouds form from gaseous water condenses as an aerosol. Eventually, solid or liquid water falls as precipitation. The evaporation of water and its condensation is called the water cycle.

Water is a simple molecule. A grade school child knows that it has the formula of $H_2O$. Oxygen, represented by O in this formula, is partially negatively charged, the two H's, hydrogen, are partially positively charged. These charges make $H_2O$ molecules stick to each other. Water also sticks to the proteins and other molecules that make up our body. For essential molecules in our body to remain functional and us to stay alive, water is required. Water is indeed part of our genetic code since DNA and RNA need it to keep active. It is part of hemoglobin (the molecule that transports oxygen from the air to every part of our body), and part of the other more than 30,000 types of protein and nucleic acid molecules in the body. The reason that soap or alcohol wipes are effective in destroying the covid virus is that soap and alcohol molecules disrupt the interaction of water with the protein, RNA and lipids that make up the virus. This destroys the virus and makes it non-infectious.

Water is needed for the circulation of blood, digestion of food, for our kidneys to remove toxic substances, and for our body to maintain temperature. Babies born with a very rare condition that prevents them from sensing heat, and thereby responding to heat and cold by sweating or shivering, typically do not live long.

Water is an integral part of the food cycle. Plants use the energy of sunlight to make sugars and other compounds from carbon dioxide and water. We eat plants, and then during metabolism, sugars are broken to carbon dioxide and water, releasing energy which allows us to live. As you are reading this, your body is actually making water, perhaps from the toast you ate for breakfast. From chemical conversion of making water (and carbon dioxide) from the food you eat, you are obtaining energy to keep you alive.

Water is a very stable molecule. It is the most common molecule observed in the universe. Seventy-one percent of the earth's surface is covered by water.

**Water as a symbol of life in the Old Testament**

Water is deeply and profoundly symbolic in the Bible. The Israelites were living in a dry, hot climate — the necessity to obtain water was a constant concern in their lives. And preoccupation with water is reflected in the Holy Scriptures. The <u>first</u> book of the Bible and the second verse, Genesis 1:2 states that the spirit of God was hovering over the water. Some scholars regard this as the first example of God the Holy Spirit in the Bible. But the recognition that water is required for creation could also be implied in this verse.

In Genesis 2:10-14, the rivers in the Garden of Eden are described. Four rivers are named, the Pishon, Gihon, Tigris and Euphrates. Specific details of rivers are given: it was important to the writer to specify exactly where the rivers ran.

In Revelation, in the <u>last</u> chapter of the Bible, the picture of Eden is reprised with a new vision of a river of water of life:

*"And he showed me a **river of water of life**, bright as crystal, proceeding out of the throne of God, and of the Lamb in the middle of the street". (Revelation 22: 1).*

From beginning to end, the Bible uses water as a symbol. And, through-out the saga of the Israelites from the time of Abraham to Jesus there are constant examples of thirst and the necessity of water.

Here is an incident about Moses (Exodus 15:22-25):

*[22] Then Moses led Israel from the Red Sea and they went into the Desert of Shur. For three days they traveled in the desert without finding water. [23] When they came to Marah, they could not drink its water because it was bitter. (That is why the place is called Marah. [24] So the people grumbled against Moses, saying, "What are we to drink?" [25] Then Moses cried out to the Lord, and the Lord showed him a piece of wood. He threw it into the water, and the **water became fit to drink**.*

About 700 years later, the theme of water remains when Isaiah (33:16) gives assurance those who walk righteously:

*they are the ones who will dwell on the heights,*
*whose refuge will be the mountain fortress. Their bread will be supplied, and **water will not fail them**.*

This poem expresses certainty that the Lord will maintain the righteous to be safe, to have food, and water.

The relationship of God to us is poetically expressed as our relationship to water in the Psalms. Psalm 1:3 recognizes that plants need water to live:

*"That person is like a tree planted by streams of water, which yields its fruit in season and whose leaf does not wither—whatever they do prospers."*

Psalm 42:1-2 forms the basis of a favorite hymn with image of a deer panting for water:

*1 As the deer pants for streams of water, so my soul pants for you, O God. 2 My soul thirsts for God, for the living God. When can I go and meet with God?*

Just as we need water to live, we need God to thrive.

**Baptism in the New Testament**

In the new testament, the use of water for purification culminates in Baptism. The Synoptic Gospels (Mark, Matthew and Luke) describe the baptism of Jesus by John the Baptist.

This is the description from Matthew, 3:13-17:

*13 Then Jesus came from Galilee to the Jordan to be baptized by John. 14 But John tried to deter him, saying, "I need to be baptized by you, and do you come to me?"*

*15 Jesus replied, "Let it be so now; it is proper for us to do this to fulfill all righteousness." Then John consented.*

*16 As soon as Jesus was baptized, he went up out of the water. At that moment heaven was opened, and he saw the Spirit of God descending like a dove and alighting on him.*

*17 And a voice from heaven said, "This is my Son, whom I love; with him I am well pleased."*

In none of the accounts from the three Synoptic Gospels is there an indication that the disciples express surprise at baptism. A long familiarity with purification by water appears to be part of their cultural background. They understood the symbolism.

After Jesus's death and resurrection, the apostles described baptism in more cosmic terms. Baptism is equated to the resurrection of Jesus. 1 Peter 3:21-22 states:

> [21] *and this water symbolizes baptism that now saves you also—not the removal of dirt from the body but the pledge of a clear conscience toward God.[e] It saves you by the resurrection of Jesus Christ,* [22] *who has gone into heaven and is at God's right hand—with angels, authorities and powers in submission to him.*

Jesus's baptism is given meaning in John 1, where John the Baptist makes clear that whereas he baptizes with water, Jesus baptizes with the Holy Spirit:

> [32] *Then John gave this testimony: "I saw the Spirit come down from heaven as a dove and remain on him.* [33] *And I myself did not know him, but the one who sent me to baptize with water told me, 'The man on whom you see the Spirit come down and remain is the one who will **baptize***

*__with the Holy Spirit.__ ' [34] I have seen and I testify that this is God's Chosen One.*

Baptism is not something done in secret but it is usually done publicly. Baptism is necessary for the spiritual life of the entire community — Jew, Gentile, slave or free — as we see in Corinthians 12:13:

*For we were all baptized by one Spirit so as to form one body—whether Jews or Gentiles, slave or free—and we were all given the one Spirit to drink.*

In this passage, the phrase "one Spirit to drink" beautifully emphasizes symbolic relationship between the Holy Spirit and water.

### Water as purification in the Biblical times

Water is required for us to keep clean, and, for us Americans, cleaning and sanitation is the major use of water. The EPA (Environmental Protection Agency) estimates that the typical family use about 300 gallons/ day. Of that 24% is used by the toilet, 20% in the shower and 17% by clothes washer.

The people who observed John the Baptist also used water for cleaning. They could have extrapolated to understand the symbolism of immersion in water. In Exodus 30:18–28, when God was giving Moses plans for the construction of the tabernacle, He instructed Moses to have a wash basin made for the priests to use before approaching the altar. Solomon's temple had containers of water called "Sea" for ceremonial washing (1 Kings 7; 2 Chronicles 4).

However, ritual bathing (as opposed to washing) as part of a religious ceremony is not an old tradition in Israel's history. Only at approximately the second to first century BCE, at the time of John the Baptist, does ritual bathing appear to become a matter of worship.

Ritual bathing in Judaism is called Mikvah. Before approximately 100-200 BCE, there are no known written sources, nor any archaeology evidence showing that Mikvah was practiced. Now, several hundred mikvahs dating from about this time have been identified in present-day Israel and in the lands of the Jewish diaspora.

King Herod the Great built The Masada, a fortification overlooking the Dead Sea, between 37 and 31 BCE. A Mikvah was identified in its ruins in 1963. (King Herod was the Jewish King recorded in the Bible who killed boy babies at the time Jesus was born. King Harold was near death at that time; he was born at 72 BCE, so his reign was mostly prior to Jesus' birth).

A 2000 year-old ritual mikvah was found near Hannaton in Israel in 2020.

A Jewish minority group, the Essenes, lived in Qumran, a site near the Dead Sea where the Dead Sea Scrolls were found. The Essenes lived in a communal monastic lifestyle that had strict membership requirements, rules, and rituals, including ritual bathing. Qumran has many ritual bathing pools. A large Miqvah has been uncovered outside of the Essene Synagogue site in the Essene quarter of Jerusalem. John the Baptist and the Essenes lived at the same time and in about the same area. Scholars have debated whether John the Baptist could have been a member of the Essenes. I believe that the consensus is that he was not. But, some things that the Essenes believed may have been incorporated into the New Testament. There was a belief that coming out of the Mikvah was like being "born again".

The water that was used in a Mikvah had to be "living water" which meant flowing water. This could be water from the ocean, a river, a spring or rainwater. It could not be water that was stored in a vessel. The distinction of living water versus non-living water was made earlier by the prophets. In Jeremiah 17:13:

*O Lord, the hope of Israel,*

*All who forsake You will be put to shame.*

*Those who turn away on earth will be written down,*

*Because they have forsaken the fountain of **living water**,*

*even the Lord.*

In Zechariah 14:8-9:

*And in that day **living waters** will flow out of Jerusalem, half of them toward the eastern sea and the other half toward the western sea; it will be in summer as well as in winter. And the Lord will be king over all the earth; in that day the Lord will be the only one, and His name the only one.*

John the Baptist baptized in the Jorden River, i.e. living water because it is flowing. The Jews at the time of John the Baptist had the knowledge of what living water was, and scriptures records that they flocked to see John the Baptist. They understood the symbolism of baptism.

**Ritual baths during the time of Christ**

A question is why did the Jews start to use ritual baths around 100 years BCE? We point out that Jews were not the only people who practiced ritual bathing. In the summer of 332 BCE, Palestine was conquered by the Greek general, Alexander the Great. The people of Israel became part of the Greek world. Greek influence is strong.  It was at this time that the Hebrew religious writings which comprise our first five books of the Old Testament were translated into Greek. The writers of the New Testament spoke Greek, as can be seen by the fact that the New Testament is written in this language. Greek spa-like installations are found around the Mediterranean. Many of these baths were dedicated to Asclepius, the Greek god of medicine and healing, and some contained minerals which were considered to be medicinal.

In 63 BCE, the land of Israel was taken from the Greeks by the Romans. During the entire time of the New Testament, the area of Israel was a vassal state of Rome. The reason that Mikvah became popular during this time may not be an indication of change of faith, but in part due to advance of technology.  The Romans, engineers *par excellence,* knew how to transport water and to build baths.  Their aqueducts are still standing and marvels to see. The Jews had a long tradition of using water as a symbol of purification, and therefore the adaptation of baths was not a strange or new thing.

This can be analogous with the use of PowerPoint during church services.  PowerPoint was not used during my childhood, simply because it had not be invented yet. No change in religious beliefs caused the sudden use of PowerPoint — only change in technology.

Many Roman baths in Europe lasted until the Black Plague, in about the mid 1300's, when their use declined because people thought that they might be transmitting plague. But, here and there, you can still find Roman baths. I had the good fortune to visit the Roman baths in Budapest, Hungary and at Bath, England. Archeological ruins of the Pool of Bethesda have been excavated. I suspect that the Pool of Bethesda looked and functioned similar to the bath I saw in England. Google "Roman Bath England" for pictures.

The Romans did not understand the origin of hot springs, and they attributed the mysterious upwelling of water as evidence that **the gods** were riling up the water. A story of hot springs at the Pool of Bethesda near Jerusalem says that **angels** riled up the water.

The account of the Pool of Bethesda is given in John 5:

*5 After this there was a feast of the Jews, and Jesus went up to Jerusalem. 2 Now there is in Jerusalem by the Sheep Gate a pool, which is called in Hebrew, Bethesda, having five porches. 3 In these lay a great multitude of sick people, blind, lame, paralyzed, waiting for the moving of* *the water. 4 For an **angel** went down at a certain time into the pool and stirred up the water; then whoever stepped in first, after the stirring of the water, was made well of whatever disease he had. 5 Now a certain man was there who had an infirmity thirty-eight years. 6 When Jesus saw him lying there, and knew that he already had been in that condition a long time, He said to him, "Do you want to be made well?"*

*7 The sick man answered Him, "Sir, I have no man to put me into the pool when the water is stirred up; but while I am coming, another steps down before me." 8 Jesus said to him, "Rise, take up your bed and walk." 9 And immediately the man was made well, took up his bed, and walked..*

Although Baptism is not recorded in the Old Testament, events in the Old Testament were interpreted by early Christians as being likened to baptism. Paul equated the passing of Israel through the Red Sea on the final Day of Unleavened Bread, with baptism in 1 Corinthians 10:1-2.

*For I do not want you to be ignorant of the fact, brothers and sisters, that our ancestors were all under the cloud and that they all passed through the sea. 2 They were all **baptized into Moses** in the cloud and in the sea. 3 They all* *ate the same spiritual food 4 and drank the same spiritual drink; for they drank from the spiritual rock that accompanied them, and that rock was Christ.*

**Today, all three religions based upon Abraham use water in ritual cleaning**

Mikvah, the Jewish water purification rite, continues to be used during our times. The practice of Mikvah has quite complex rules, at least it seems so to me. But, basically, the rules harken back to Leviticus 15 where purification laws for Israelites are given. Under many conditions — contact with a corpse or discharge from body, ritual cleaning was called for. In Leviticus 15:15

*'Now when the man with the discharge becomes cleansed from his discharge, then he shall count off for himself seven days for his cleansing; he shall then wash his clothes and bathe his body in running water and will become clean.*

A close friend of mine married a man from an observant Jewish family. Before his family accepted her, she took a Mikvah as ritual cleaning. In our area, Denver has two Mikvahs and Boulder has one. The Boulder Mikvah is particularly beautiful and stylistically incorporates rocks in a form of a landscape. Google "Mikvah Boulder CO" for a picture.

Besides Judaism and Christianity, the other Abrahamic religion is Islam, began around 600 AD with the prophet Mohammed. Islam also has bathing incorporated into its rituals. When traveling in Moslem countries I observed men washing themselves before entering mosques. As far as I can tell, the requirements for Islam and Jewish purification rites are similar and both are based upon Leviticus.

Baptism is used in all Christian churches. Details of baptism differ among denominations, but I think that in most Christian denominations, baptism is more of an affirmation of faith and acknowledgment of being a member of the Christian Church, than the ritualistic cleansing of Judaism and Islam. Some churches have infant baptism, other have only adult baptism; some use immersion, some sprinkling of water, some pouring of water. In Greek Orthodox churches children are baptized at age around 1 year to 18 months. The child is dunked under the water three times, symbolizing God the Father, the Son, and Holy Spirit. In Calvinistic churches and the Catholic Church children are considered to be born sinful. Being sinful at birth is the doctrine of Original Sin, developed by St.

Augustine of Hippo, which states that since our ancestors (i.e., Adam and Eve) sinned, then all people are sinful. In these churches, baptism is encouraged upon or shortly after birth to acknowledge that the child is now accepted in the community born of believers and dedicated to Jesus. Other churches only accept adult baptism. In this case, baptism is more a symbol of the person's acknowledgment of faith in Jesus.

In most churches, the baptismal font is conspicuously displayed. Sometimes the baptismal font is in the front of the church, near the altar. In other churches the font is in the back, so that you walk by it when you enter the sanctuary. In some Renaissance churches the Baptistry is a separate building away from the main sanctuary. The baptistry at the cathedral in Pisa, Italy is a separate building from the main sanctuary, and it has a beautiful marble interior. Google "pisa baptistery interior" for pictures.

**Final comments**

In some aspects, we look at water differently than the Biblical writers. We know about the water cycle: water evaporating to eventually fall again as precipitation. We know about water being required for metabolism and our body functions. We know that water molecules are part of the proteins, DNA and RNA that we need to survive. These things the Biblical writers would not have known, but we share with them the knowledge that water is essential for life. We need water to keep our bodies alive and we need water for cleaning.

In writing this, I emphasized water's role in cleaning and hygiene. The act of bathing is symbolic of repentance and purification from sin.

King David poignantly wrote Psalm 51:7 when he was repenting for committing adultery with Bathsheba:

*Purge me with hyssop, and I shall be clean; wash me, and I shall be whiter than snow.*

In John 3:5 Jesus told the disciples:

*"Very truly I tell you, no one can enter the kingdom of God unless they are born of water and the Spirit."*

Water is used as a key symbol of the Holy Spirit throughout the Bible. It is apparently colorless, and apparently a simple molecule. But its presence is required for our life in many obvious ways and in ways that we may not be aware. When the disciples of Jesus came upon John the Baptist, they already had a cultural background that allowed them to understand the significance of baptism. They could understand that water is essential to our physical life, just as God's grace is essential to our spiritual life. The symbol of water is perhaps best illustrated by Jesus's conversation with the Samaritan woman recorded in John 4:

> *6Jacob's well was there, and Jesus, tired as he was from the journey, sat down by the well. It was about noon. 7 When a Samaritan woman came to draw water, Jesus said to her, "Will you give me a drink?" ….*
>
> *9The Samaritan woman said to him, "You are a Jew and I am a Samaritan woman. How can you ask me for a drink?" …. 10Jesus answered her, "If you knew the gift of God and who it is that asks you for a drink, you would have asked him and **he would have given you living water.**" 11 "Sir," the woman said, "you have nothing to draw with and the well is deep. Where can you get this living water? 12 Are you greater than our father Jacob, who gave us the well and drank from it himself, as did also his sons and his livestock?"*
>
> *13Jesus answered, "Everyone who drinks this water will be thirsty again, 14but whoever drinks the water I give them will never thirst. Indeed, **the water I give them will become in them a spring of water welling up to eternal life.**"*

### Chapter 5

# Communion: Flesh and Blood

No matter how rich or powerful we are, all of us will experience losing loved ones to death. And all of us, no matter whether we deny it or not, must realize that we too will die. Communion celebrates the death and resurrection of Christ. Communion is a meal in which bread, symbolizing Christ's flesh, and wine, symbolizing Christ's blood, is consumed. In this essay, we are going to focus on the revolutionary aspects of communion.

## Passover lamb

The crucifixion and resurrection Jesus is the central tenet of Christian beliefs. Jesus's sacrifice—his spilled blood — atones for our sins. Before the events of crucifixion, Jesus and his disciples had a meal together to celebrate the holiday of Passover. Passover is the most sacred feast of the Jewish religious year. It commemorates the final plague on Egypt when the firstborn of the Egyptians died.  Israelites who sprinkled blood of a lamb on their door frames were spared and were able to exit from Egypt (Exodus 12).  To celebrate their deliverance they had a feast eating Lamb.

Jesus was to deliver people from sin, by his sacrifice. Just as a lamb was sacrificed at Passover, Jesus was to be the Lamb sacrificed for our sins.

### Lord's Supper in the Bible

Matthew 26 records events at the Lord's Supper as follows:

> [26] *While they were eating, Jesus took bread, and when he had given thanks, he broke it and gave it to his disciples, saying, "**Take and eat; this is my body.**" [27] Then he took a cup, and when he had given thanks, he gave it to them, saying, "**Drink from it, all of you. 28 This is my blood of the covenant, which is poured out for many for the forgiveness of sins.** [29] I tell you, I will not drink from this fruit of the vine from now on until that day when I drink it new with you in my Father's kingdom.*

I am going to focus on the eating of body and drinking of blood. What would the disciples thought about the eating of their teacher, Jesus, and drinking his blood?

**What is flesh?**

The eating of flesh is the first element of communion. Flesh is the soft tissue surrounding our bones and over our abdomen. It is composed mostly of fat and muscle. The Bible has no prohibition against eating either fat or muscle. Fat is associated with abundance. Nehemiah reminds the Israelites that God gave them the land of Canaan where they became prosperous. Nehemiah 9:25:

> *And they took strong cities, and a fat land, and possessed houses full of all goods, wells digged, vineyards, and olive yards, and fruit trees in abundance: so they did eat, and were filled, and **became fat, and delighted themselves in thy great goodness**.*

Most of us are separated from the raising and slaughtering of livestock, but ancient people were directly involved with the production of food. We politely prefer not to dissect meat that we are eating in order to identify a particular muscle. I have never heard anyone say "Oh, gosh, this gastrocnemius muscle is very nicely flavored" while eating a steak in an upscale restaurant.

Would the ancient writers understand that meat is muscle that is cooked? I think that they probably understood this. They knew of the importance of muscle. In Isaiah 48:4:

*For I knew how stubborn you were; your neck muscles were iron, your forehead was bronze.*

The Israelites could identify heart, liver, kidneys, bones and other organs, even if they did not know their functions. The above verse suggests that they knew the function of muscle.

**Meaning of flesh in the Bible**

In the Bible, flesh can mean the corporate body, rather than the spiritual part of a human. In Psalm 73:26, the flesh means that the body is failing by temptation, but God can give strength and portion (i.e. destiny):

*My flesh and my heart may fail, but God is the strength of my heart and my portion forever.*

Matthew 26 describes the events immediately after the Last Supper. These events occurred in the Garden of Gethsemane and include  the betrayal of Jesus and his arrest, before his trial and crucifixion. He tells the disciples to watch and pray while he withdrew and prayed. He says in Matthew 26:

> [41] *"Watch and pray so that you will not fall into temptation. The spirit is willing, but the flesh is weak."*

The disciples were tired — their flesh needed sleep.

### Blood then and now

Jews have strict dietary laws and they would not have drunk blood. Genesis 9:4 states: "But you shall not eat flesh with its life, that is, its blood." The prohibition against eating blood is very strict. To this day, Kosher meats are prepared by bleeding the animal to remove blood. Similar methods are used to prepare Halal meats in Islamic religious practice. The lamb prepared for Passover meal would have been bled, so that the meat would not contain blood.

Like many other traditions in the Bible, the prohibition to consume blood has an origin upon scientific observation. Early people could observe that both we and a plant, say a tree, are alive. But we have a soul and thoughts, and a tree does not. What is the difference? Trees do not have blood; we do. If we bleed excessively life ebbs out of us. It was a logical conclusion to think that blood might be the origin of soul.  When we read "blood" in the Bible, it often means actual blood but it can also mean the life force of someone, in Hebrew *nephesh*, meaning "soul, self, life".

This view of blood is retained in our language idioms. "Bad blood" is an idiom used to indicate bitterness or antagonism; we now understand that it means nothing about actual blood. "It's in his blood" means that he is born prone to do something.  "Blood brothers" refers to loyalty between people, not actual kinship.

Our view of blood is quite different from ancient people's. We know that blood transports oxygen to every cell in the body.  Most of the cells within blood are red blood cells. These cells contain hemoglobin, which binds oxygen in our lungs and releases oxygen to every tissue in the body. Red blood cells do not contain DNA, which is the genetic material required for cells to duplicate. Red blood cells do not contain mitochondria which are the part of the cell that converts food to most of its energy. Blood is one of the least "live" tissue.

Most Christians donate blood for blood transfusion without qualms, and, if we need blood, we would accept a blood transfusion. Blood have different types, which arise due to different proteins and sugars on the membranes of red blood cells. As long as blood type is matched, we can have a blood transfusion without fear of rejection due to an immune response.

Many of us Americans have a cultural abhorrence of eating, drinking or even thinking about blood. About a quarter of Americans menstruate monthly, but this fact is carefully hidden. Our fear of eating blood arises in spite of the fact that most countries of our ancestors use blood in soup and in sausages. Blood and flesh are healthy foods, and some peoples of the world use them as their major food source. The traditional meal of the Maasai people of Tanzania is milk mixed with blood, occasionally supplemented by meat. The Inuit people of the Arctic historically ate blubber and meat and occasional birds and eggs. Without eating fruits and vegetables, these two groups of people are healthy.

**Human sacrifice**

Now we look at the heritage of Jesus and the disciples. Sacrifice of humans is accepted in the story of Abraham preparing to sacrifice his son, Isaac. That story of Abraham's acquiescence to God's command to sacrifice Isaac was used in the early Christian church as an example of faith (Hebrews

11:17) and of obedience (James 2:21). Still, sacrificing your child is certainly contrary to what we now think how a parent should act.

The sacrifice of Abraham's son seems to be an exceptional occurrence overall, however. In the Bible, both human sacrifice and cannibalism are atrocities, brutal examples of the very worst that people can do. When the Bible talks about human sacrifice, it usually highlights the fact that it occurs under extreme conditions. In Deuteronomy 28:52-57, there is a long list of curses for disobedience to God. Eating one's own children is listed as a curse in these verses. Another example, the Bible describes King Ahaz of Judah as a bad king by describing how he "made offerings in the Valley of the Son of Hinnom and burned his sons as an offering" (2 Chronicles 28:3). This would show a very egregious example of evil and disobedience to God.

The prophet Micah rails against corrupt rulers, using the example of eating people to illustrate the depths of evil. He says that corrupt leaders (Micah 3:1-4):

> *"Listen, you leaders of Jacob,*
> *    you rulers of Israel.*
> *Should you not embrace justice,*
> *[2] you who hate good and love evil;*

*who tear the skin from my people*
*and the flesh from their bones;*
*³ **who eat my people's flesh**,*
*strip off their skin*
*and break their bones in pieces;*
***who chop them up like meat for the pan**,*
*like flesh for the pot?"*
*⁴ Then they will cry out to the Lord,*
*but he will not answer them.*
*At that time he will hide his face from them*
*because of the evil they have done.*

In the above passage eating and actual cooking of flesh is described. The criticism of Micah towards the corrupt rulers of his time is particularly harsh, even for us who are used to hearing extreme criticisms and ridicule of our leaders in contentious times of social media.

So, while cannibalism is part of human sacrifice in some cultures, the Bible mentions human sacrifice to highlight the times when Jews were following false gods and when people were disobeying God's commandments. Cannibalism is considered to be a particularly abhorrent behavior of disobedience.

**Communion, Mass, Eucharist.**

Christians celebrate the death and resurrection of Jesus with a ritual meal of bread and wine. The title of this sacrament varies among churches. "Mass" is used in Roman Catholic and Episcopal churches, "Eucharist" is used in other churches, "The Sacrament" is used in Mormon churches, and the Presbyterian and Reformed churches of my background use the term "Communion". The symbols of communion are bread, representing Jesus' flesh, and wine, representing Jesus' blood. All three synoptic gospels (Matthew, Mark and Luke) describe the last meal they had with Jesus.

Notably, the meal that they were eating was the Passover dinner. We go back to Exodus 12. Passover celebrated the deliverance of the Israelites from Egypt when blood of a lamb was painted over the doors of houses. We note that blood was just not a marker - an "x" written with a piece of chalk would not do. Blood represented the soul — the essence of life — of the lamb.

There are many examples of Jesus blood and flesh being linked to the Passover lamb. For example, John (John 1:29) tells what John the Baptist says when he first sees Jesus:

After the miracle of feeding 5,000 people, the apostle John (John 6:53-59) records that Jesus explains that we need to eat his flesh and drink his blood.  Here is the scripture:

[53] Jesus said to them, "Very truly I tell you, unless you eat the flesh of the Son of Man and drink his blood, you have no life in you. [54] Whoever eats my flesh and drinks my blood has eternal life, and I will raise them up at the last day. [55] For my **flesh is real food and my blood is real drink**. [56] Whoever eats my flesh and drinks my blood remains in me, and I in them. [57] Just as the living Father sent me and I live because of the Father, so the one who feeds on me will live because of me. [58] This is the bread that came down from heaven. Your ancestors ate manna and died, but whoever feeds on this bread will live forever."

Paul likens Jesus to the Passover lamb in 1 Corinthians 5:7:

[7] Get rid of the old yeast, so that you may be a new unleavened batch—as you really are. For **Christ, our Passover lamb**, has been sacrificed.

It is notable that during the Last Supper meal, Jesus foresaw his death. In Mark 14:

> [22] *While they were eating, Jesus took bread, and when he had given thanks, he broke it and gave it to his disciples, saying, "Take it;* ***this is my body.****"*[23]*Then he took a cup, and when he had given thanks, he gave it to them, and they all drank from it.* [24] *"****This is my blood*** *of the covenant, which is poured out for many," he said to them.* [25] *"Truly I tell you, I will not drink again from the fruit of the vine until that day when I drink it new in the kingdom of God."*

This passage seems quite explicit of eating Jesus's body and drinking His blood.

### Ancient funeral rites

The disciples did not understand what Jesus was saying about Jesus' impending death.  But the Jews also were prohibited to drink blood or eat people. Perhaps the statements of drinking blood and eating flesh would have been confusing to them too. We can look at other cultures.

Where the person has gone after death is a mystery approached by all people over all times. Archeologist have studied the remains of ancient peoples. In ancient graves the remains of people are found buried with flowers and personal items, a tradition that we still sometimes follow. Sometimes the items are thought to be used by the person in the afterlife. Other times the items show love and respect to the person who died.

Another funeral rite found by archeologists is more unfamiliar to us — that is cannibalism in funeral rituals. In Gouch's cave in Somerset, England, human bones from 14,700 years ago are found. These bones show evidence of being chewed upon by other humans. In this cave many animal bones were also found, so the researchers surmised that these people were not starving, and therefore did not resort to cannibalism due to lack of food. Rather they suggest that eating part of the loved one who died was a way to pass the "power" or "spirit" of that person on to the living.

In our times the Fore people of New Guinea carry out such a ritual. In this case, the dying person would let their preference known how their body would be disposed after death. The belief is that ritual consumption of the deceased person allows somehow the spirit of the deceased to be passed on to their loved ones. It is considered to be an honor to be the designated eater of flesh. Some groups in the Amazon are also known to consume the deceased.

The consuming of human flesh is not accepted in our culture. The most beloved president of the United States is arguably George Washington. His body was not eaten after his death. The United Kingdom is a monarchy.  After the monarch's death there is no actual or ritual consumption of the body. Only in communion do we have such a meal.

**The idea of equating communion and cannibalism is not new**

In the early days of Christianity, the Romans persecuted the Christians, the major reason being that Christianity challenged Roman religion and authority.  It may have been more than that. Tacitus, a Roman Senator about 100 AD, characterized "Christian abominations" that may have been based on the rumors in Rome that during the Eucharist rituals Christians ate the body and drank the blood of their God. The Roman interpretation of the ritual was that Christians were cannibals.  If we knew nothing about Christianity and we heard about communion, we might come to the same conclusion.

Many people lost their lives in England and in Germany in the aftermath of the Reformation over the question of the meaning of communion.  If the words of Jesus indicate the literal presence of Christ's body and blood in bread and wine (trans-substantiation), then are we eating Jesus's body? (A way around the charge of cannibalism has been to say that Jesus is living, therefore, of course, we are not eating his body).

You can read the scriptures yourself to see whether you agree that Jesus is saying that you are actually eating flesh and drinking blood, or whether it is symbolic. Passages to be looked at are: Matthew 26:17-30; Mark 14:12-25; Luke 22:7-20; and John 13:1-30. Paul writes about it in 1 Corinthians 11: 23 – 26. Since Paul wrote before the gospels this passage would be the first written account. Looking at various translations might help make up your mind. You can also decide whether thinking about actual blood and flesh makes the ritual more meaningful to you. In doing this, you will be following what the church fathers pondered. Martin Luther thought that the communion elements actually had Jesus' blood and flesh, whereas, John Calvin said that Jesus' presence in the bread and wine is real, but a spiritual sense, not physical. I suspect that if you would take a poll of our church members the majority would agree with Ulrich Zwingli: that the bread and wine are symbols that represent the body and blood of Jesus.

**What would the disciples take Jesus's words to mean?**

So, I am coming back to the question: would the words of Jesus be understandable — and shocking — to the Disciples? Did they knew the symbolism behind eating human flesh and drinking blood?  Jesus was the sacrificial lamb, but the lamb in the Passover feast would have been prepared in a Kosher manner; it would have been bled so that people would not consume blood. As stated above, the Israelites had a long prohibition of drinking animal blood — and Jesus was telling them to drink human — His — blood.  As Jews, were the disciples confused?  For the Jews at this time, blood was equated with the essence of life,  the soul of the person.

Drinking blood and eating flesh would definitely be against the covenant made between the Jews and God in the Old Testament.

It is important to recognize that Jesus is saying that the Old Covenant is gone. Although exactly when the books of the Bible were written, the letter of Paul to the church at Corinth is likely to be one of the earliest. In 1 Corinthians 11 Paul writes::

[23] *... The Lord Jesus, on the night he was betrayed, took bread,* [24] *and when he had given thanks, he broke it and*

We are taught that Communion is to remind us of the death and resurrection of Jesus, through which he died for our sins. The writing of Paul emphasizes that Jesus' sacrifice meant that the old covenant of the Old Testament was gone.

In Sermon on the Mount (Matthew 5-7) Jesus up-ends what is thought about morality and importance of people. He states: Blessed are the poor in spirit. Blessed are those who mourn. Blessed are the meek. Love your enemies. Turn the other check and so on.

The words of Jesus in the Sermon on the Mount are radical concepts. They are opposite with what we are advised in "How to Succeed" books.

Communion is also radical. The act of communion challenges us. It requires our active participation. It is an admission of our depravity. We do not sit passively listening to a sermon, but we need to eat bread and drink wine. It is saying in the most dramatic way possible that we acknowledge that we

need Jesus to become part of us.  What we eat becomes part of
our body. We need Jesus to become part of our soul.

### Chapter 6

# Creation and the Origin of Life

What do you think is the biggest barrier between science and Christianity? I asked several people this question and they were of the opinion that the theory of evolution is the major off-putting barrier.

Evolution is currently the basic underlying theory of biology, just as the atomic theory is the current foundation of chemistry and continental drift theory is the underlying basis of geology.

### Creation in the Bible

Many writers have attacked evolution from a Biblical point of view and they usually attack by finding some "flaw" in evolutionary theory. I think that this is counter-productive.

Instead I will start with what the Bible states about creation and ask what we learn about creation in the Bible.

The first two chapters of Genesis may seem hard to read. For instance, what do we make of Genesis 1: 27 which states that mankind, male and female, were made of the same time, in the image of God? In contrast, Genesis 2:22, states that Eve was made from a rib of Adam. Which is it? This seems like a contradiction and deserves further examination.

In Genesis 1-Genesis 2:4, the sequence for creation is:

Day 1: Heavens and earth, light, divided light and darkness (verses. 1-5)

Day 2: Expanse between waters (v. 6-8)

Day 3: dry ground (v. 10)

vegetation (v. 11)

seed plants and fruit trees (9-13)

Day 4: sun and moon (v. 14-18)

Day 5: animals in sea and birds (v. 20-21)

wild animals and livestock (v. 25)

Day 6: **mankind, male and female** (v. 27).

Creation in Genesis 1 is orderly, occurring in divisions of six days. Mankind is the last thing created.

No such time stipulation is found in Genesis 2. In Genesis 2:4 and following:

Heavens and earth

plants

rain

**man was made from dust** (v. 7)

a garden made with trees (v. 9)

river to water garden (10)

man commanded not to eat from tree of knowledge of good and evil (16)

wild animals and birds (v. 19)

**woman made from Man's rib** (v. 22).

The time that it took for creation seems different in the two stories. The first story says that creation occurred in six days. Sometimes this time scale is explained away by quoting 2 Peter 3:8: "One day is with the Lord as a thousand years, and a thousand years as one day." The second story does not specify the length of time.

But it is harder to explain away differences in sequence of events. In Genesis 1:27 male and female were created at the <u>same time</u> at the <u>end</u> of creation. In Genesis 2:7 man was made near the <u>beginning</u> of creation, before trees, animals and birds. The status of women in the Bible is of particular concern these days. In the second story man was made from dust. Then (Genesis 2:22) woman was made from man's rib.

Of course, we are not the first to notice discrepancies between the two stories. During Medieval times, Jewish writing and folklore described Eve as the second wife of Adam. This got around the problem that Genesis 1:27 clearly states that male and female were created at the same time, and Genesis 2:22 which says Eve was made from Adam's rib. In folklore, the first wife was named Lilith, and she was evil. She was an incarnation of lust, leading men to sin and she killed babies. By concluding that Adam had two wives, with Eve being the "good" second wife, the discrepancy between Genesis 1:27 and Genesis 2:22 could be reconciled.

You can find some other, some rather innovative attempts to reconcile discrepancies in the Biblical account on the internet. But, like the addition of Lilith to justify one discrepancy, additional details are added to the Biblical account in many attempts found on the Internet. We do not want to add things to Bible stories. Also, we do not want to try to force the Bible to explain facts.

But perhaps we are reading the Bible wrong. There have been explanations for apparent contradiction. One explanation, and the explanation that is probably now most accepted, is that there are <u>two</u> stories of creation in the Bible. So, for these reasons, we will examine the explanation of two creation stories.

The first creation story starts in Genesis 1:1 and the second one starts in Genesis 2:4. When the scripture is laid out side by side, it certainly looks like two creation stories.

So, if there are two creation stories, what are the two stories trying to tell us? Are there truths in the stories that we will miss if we try to force these stories to conform to each other and to what we know of science?

To me, the first story emphasizes the glory of creation. It leads us think about the glories of the earth and sea, of the sky above, of the animals around us. When you are in the mountains, and you look at the beauty of nature, and at night see millions of stars in the Milky Way above, you are in awe. The beauty and magnificence of the world leads you to think of God.

In the second story, God is more personal. He made a beautiful garden for Adam, and, when he saw that Adam was not happy, he made Eve for him. I think this is the aspect of God you are thinking about when your child is sick, and you are driving to the emergency room. Then you are praying to a God who has a personal interest in you and your family, and will act on your behalf. I think that this is also an aspect of God you are thinking about when you give thanks at Thanksgiving dinner, surrounded by your loved ones and when you are aware of your blessings.

The second story also has man interacting with the world more. In Genesis 2:19-20, God instructs man to name all the wild animals and all the birds. Verse 19 says that God brought them to the man to see what he would name each animal. This sounds like God is curious and even playful in seeing how man would respond to creation. (Did God say "Let's make a giraffe and see what man names it"?).  Naming of animals is important activity. A first step in scientific inquiry is to name the organism or phenomenon that you observe.

By taking both accounts of creation, I think we get a better understanding of our relationship with God. If we try to force the Bible to account for scientific observable facts, we lose the main point. It closes our mind to what is really important in this scripture.

How did two stories of creation enter in the Bible? A suggestion is that the Bible was written after the Kingdom broke apart, and Judah and Israel existed separate from each other.  The two parts of the Divided Kingdom had slightly different creation stories. Both contain Truths, and both were included in the Bible.

**Evolution**

I should say something about evolution. Evolution is not an easy topic, and it is easily subjected to misinterpretation. However, this theory greatly aids the study of biology since it helps to explain relationships between species. There are so many species and life is so diverse! I studied a protein called cytochrome $c$. All the living things that you see right now has cytochrome $c$ — plants, the cat laying on the couch, a fly buzzing around, the fungus between your toes causing athlete's feet (if you are so unlucky), yeast in the sandwich bread you are eating, and in nearly all cells of your body. This protein is very much the same in all species. But you are more related to your cat, than to a plant or a fly. So, we can predict that cytochrome $c$ in you and the cat are also more closely related. This makes it easier to study cytochrome $c$; if we were to devise a drug that would act upon cytochrome $c$, we might expect that drug would affect us and the cat more than the fly. We do not need to study the protein in all living things to see how this protein functions in different living things.

Charles Darwin (1809 – 1882) and Alfred Wallace (1823-1913) independently proposed evolutionary theory in the middle of the 19th century. Darwin's book *On the Origin of Species* was published in 1859. Evolutionary theory immediately got people's attention. A famous debate in 1860 between Thomas Huxley (1825-1895) and Archbishop Wilberforce occurred in 1860. Other debates followed between "Creationists" and "Evolutionists" over the years. Initially, detractors of evolution made the point that the "missing link" between the common ancestor and humans was missing. But, by now many fossils of what appears to be precursors to *Homo Sapiens* have been found. So this seems like a lesser problem.

The study of genetics now seems to be the area of interest for evolution. At the time, Darwin and Wallace proposed evolution they had no idea how mutations - changes - in species occurred. In 1944, Oswald Avery, Colin Macleod, and Maclyn McCarty published evidence of DNA is the genetic material of organisms. In 1953 the structure of DNA was elucidated by James Watson and Francis Crick based upon data of Rosalind Franklin. In 1990, the Human Genome Project (HGP), began to decode the human genome. Researchers from around the world began sequencing and mapping more than 3 billion DNA letters. By 2003, the map was "concluded," however there were some gaps in the sequence. On March 31, 2020 scientists published a paper where the sequence of the gaps were filled. The map now complete with 3.055-billion base-pair sequences.

Any alteration in DNA will change proteins, and then the organism. There are many ways that DNA can be altered. In point mutation one base pair (the unit of DNA) is altered and this results in one amino acid change in the protein. The base of DNA can be chemically changed, say by a carcinogen, or changed by UV light, or by radioactive rays — many ways. But there are other ways DNA changes too. Frame shift is when one whole segment of DNA shifts, causing a large change in proteins. There may be deletion of part of the DNA; such an event has been suggested to occur in wolves, when gene deletion produced the common dog. There may be duplication of part of the DNA strand. It is recently recognized that DNA contains pseudogenes. These pseudogenes look like the sequence of genes but they do not make protein. The pseudogenes can independently mutate. One gene can affect the expression of other genes. An exciting recent development is the recognition that base pairs can be inserted into DNA of the human genome by viruses. This can promote tumor development, including in HBV and HPV viruses.

Science is never written in stone. If experimental data contradict evolution, this theory will be thrown out and replaced by another. But, for right now, evolution is the operating theory. It is consistent with fossil records, with anatomy, with molecular biology, genetics, biochemistry and embryology. It is predictive in how living organisms live and act. It explains the amazing diversity of living things. In our present pandemic, evolution has helped us understand how the coronavirus has mutated and what we should do to help prevent us from disease.

Detractors of evolution will often put forward a "aha!" example why organisms did not evolve, often based upon statistics. But there have always ways to debunk their so-called proofs that purport showing evolution is incorrect. This approach is also dangerous, I fear, because what if evolution would be definitely proved to be correct? Would they lose their faith? But, God still exists; it was only our interpretation of the Bible story that was incorrect.

The evolution/religion conflict is not the first time there has been a science/ religion conflict. Galileo Galilei (1564 – 1642) put forward the idea, based upon the work of Nicolaus Copernicus (1473-1543), that the earth rotated and circles the sun. To the people at that time, this seemed contradictory to the Bible. For example, Ecclesiastes 1:5 seems to imply that the sun rotated around the earth. Then as now, people wanted humans to be the center of things, and so they wanted earth to be the center of the universe. Galileo was placed on house arrest. It took a very long time for the church to admit to its error. On October 1992, Pope John Paul II acknowledged that the Church had erred in condemning Galileo for asserting that the Earth revolves around the Sun. Pope John Paul said that we must distinguish between the words of Bible and its interpretation, a point that I find very profound.

Another evolution/religion conflict occurred at about the same time. William Harvey (1578-1657) published work demonstrating that the heart was a pump for blood circulation. Other workers had known part of the function of the heart; including workers described in Ayurveda literature from India. Harvey's paper was called "Exercitatio Anatomica de Motu Cordis et Sanguinis in Animalibus" and it was published in Latin. The first English translation did not appear until two decades later. There are 830 verses about heart in the Bible, and none of them mention that the heart is a pump. It took several decades for the idea of the heart as a pump to be accepted.

**Humans in God's creation**

Perhaps the detractors of evolution fear that humans unique position in God's creation would be lost if evolution is the case. But, the Bible does not focus on the creation of man. The Bible says that we have a humble beginning: God created man from dust (Genesis 2:7). Ecclesiastes 3:20 reminds us that we become dust:

*All go to one place; all come from dust, and all return to dust. All go to the same place; all come from dust, and to dust all return. Both go to the same place—they came from dust and they return to dust*

The over-all arc of the Bible is that God gave his Son for us — humans. The arc is not how we were created. This is the truth of the story of God's gift to man (John 3: 16-17):

*[16] For God so loved the world that he gave his one and only Son, that whoever believes in him shall not perish but have eternal life. [17] For God did not send his Son into the world to condemn the world, but to save the world through him.*

We lose sight of the truths of creation if Biblical accounts are forced upon science, and worry about details of our creation. We should not dictate to God how He choses to create life. Should we consider what evolution tells us about how we should treat God's creation? Genes, all organisms, the environment are all interconnected. We all need to cooperate with each other. This concept is especially important now, as we realize how our actions affect global warming, and the life of all species.

Just as biologists are interested in the origin of life, astronomers are interested in the origin of the universe. Looking to the skies, we encounter many, many unknowns. The current theory of the origin of the universe is the "Big Bang" theory. The universe started small and suddenly began to expand, during which time light appeared and then matter appeared. I have heard some people say that this theory is in-line with the thinking of the origin of the universe in Genesis. Genesis 1:3: "And God said: Let there be light and there was light." But, I do not accept this possible coincidence. What existed at the time of the Big Bang? Science does not know now, and the creation story in the Bible does not state what it was either (Genesis 1:2 "the earth was formless") — but it was something.

So this is my thought: that we may lose insight and truth in both the science and the Bible story if we close our minds to one or the other or try to interpret one strictly by the other. Consistent, with what Pope John Paul stated, when we read, see or hear we are always registering our interpretation of what we read, see, or hear. When we read the Bible, we are registering in our minds our interpretation of the Bible. We, including and especially myself, can be in error. The stories of creation become more meaningful when we think about what we learn from them.

Chapter **7**

# **Infectious Diseases during Bible times**

When we look at the Bible, we find descriptions of diseases and conditions familiar to us. There has always been suffering, and a question, asked by Job, and being asked continually by mankind is "Why?"

**Parasites**

We expect that our religious beliefs and practices are healthy and contribute to our well-being. But, that may not always be the case.

Having a ceremony of ritual cleaning does not mean "sanitary" or "healthy" in our way of thinking. In Chapter 4 we described ritual bathing practices. The hygiene practices of the Essenes who lived in Qumran are described in articles from Science Daily and the Jerusalem Post. Joe Zias, Curator of Archaeology and Anthropology for the Israel Antiquities

Authority, compared the age of men who were buried in cemeteries in Jericho with those buried in Qumran. There was about a 50% chance that a man in Jericho died after age 40, whereas in Qumran this number was 6%. Dr. Zias believes that the difference in longevity between Jericho and Qumran is accounted for by latrine practices and the use of Mikvah. In Qumran, the fecal matter was buried according to instructions in Deuteronomy 23:12-14:

> *[12] You must also have a place outside the camp where one may go outside. [13] You must have a spade among your equipment, and it must be, when you relieve yourself outside, you must dig there and turn and cover up your excrement. [14] For the Lord your God walks in the midst of your camp, to deliver you, and to defeat your enemies before you. Therefore, your camp must be holy, so that He does not see any indecent thing among you, and turn away from you.*

Excavation by Zias and coworkers of the latrine at Qumran found eggs from intestinal parasites, including roundworm (*Ascaris*), whipworm (*Trichuris*), tapeworm (*Taenia*) and pinworm (*Enterobius vermicularis*). It is suggested that burial of poo-poo increased the viability of these eggs. In contrast to the Essenes, Bedouins who also lived in the dry climate at the time of the Essenes (and live there now) left their feces in the sun, where the sun's ultraviolet rays and dryness of the atmosphere kills the eggs.

There was, therefore, the possibility of being infected with parasites when using the latrine at Qumran — especially if the Essene had a cut on his foot and was barefoot or wearing sandals. The problem was made worse because after using the latrine, the men were required to bath in a Mikvah. Rain water — considered living water — was used for the water in the Mikvah. Rain is sparse in this climate, and the water in the latrine could not be changed often. There would be an additional chance of getting infected with parasites — as well as bacteria — when bathing in the Mikvah.

Parasites would probably have been quite common during Biblical times. Herod Agrippa, the king of Judea during the time of Jesus, had intestinal parasites as recorded in Acts 12:23. The historian Josephus also records his death and verifies that he had worms. My physician friends put out that he may not have died from the parasites, though. He had sudden severe stomach pains, was sick with pain in his abdomen for five days, and then died. They say that his symptoms match more closely to appendicitis. This disease has been common and deadly throughout the ages.

**Amoeba in water?**

When reading the Bible — or indeed any historical work — we sometimes forget that the knowledge of microorganisms that cause disease is only recently acquired.

**Amoeba** are single cell organism which are extremely flexible because they do not have a rigid cell wall. The earliest report of an amoeboid organism was published in 1755 by August Johann Rösel von Rosenhof, whose illustrations show a freshwater amoeba, similar in appearance to the species now known as *Amoeba proteus*. Parasitic amoeba can cause dysentery, and while enterotoxic *E. Coli* is probably the most common cause of "tourista" when traveling to areas of the world with impure water, amoeba are also a possible cause of diarrhea.

Some parasitic amoeba can infect the brain. In chapter 5 the Roman Bath in Bath England was described. This water was used for bathing for almost 2000 years. In 1978 a 12 year old girl died from meningoencephalitis after swimming in the Bath. It was found that amoeba, named *Naegleria fowleri*, inhaled through her nose, caused her brain disease. The water comes from the hot springs is above the boiling point of water.

The amoeba could survive this, and now the pools are closed for swimming, soaking or drinking. Presumably these amoeba were in the water during Roman times. Why did the Romans not get sick? Now-a-days, when people go into a pool, they swim. The Romans likely just soaked, and therefore it was less probable that they breathed in amoeba-infected water. Also, it was the sick who came to soak in the Baths in England during Roman era. In those times people might not have noticed if there was additional mortality after bathing.

*Naegleria fowleri* has been found in hot springs in Japan, Europe, Utah and California. Whether this amoeba would have been been in the hot springs at Bethesda described in the Bible (John 5), is, of course, not known. I am only giving this example of when something that appears healthy may not be. I noticed that the water at the pool at Glenwood Canyon Hot Springs in Colorado is pre-treated with ozone, a reactive oxygen compound. Ozone kills amoeba, and I suspect the owners of the Glenwood Hot Springs use ozone because they are aware of possibility of infection from amoeba.

**Skin disease caused by pathogens**

There are many kinds of skin diseases. The Israelites, with emphasis on purity, were afraid of them. Conditions that cause rash include eczema, psoriasis, allergies, heat, and many pathogen infections. Bacteria, viruses, fungi and parasitic pathogens can all cause skin rashes. Commonly known skin rash from a virus include chicken pox. Examples of fungal skin infections include ring worm and jock itch. Parasitic skin infections include scabies, caused by mites, and lice. Bacterial skin infections can be caused *Staphylococcus* and *Streptococcus* bacteria. Staphylococcus infections are particularly worrisome in hospital and nursing home settings, as the bacteria has become resistant to antibiotics.

Today we can identify some diseases as coming from a particular pathogen, but there are still mystery diseases with no known etiology. Ancient people had a harder time to specify diseases. Hippocrates (c. 460 – c. 370 BC), the "Father of Medicine," called skin, flaky, discolored skin rashes as "lepra". Hebrew of the Old Testament used the word *tzaraat* as a word to describe skin diseases.

Five books of the Bible were translated from Hebrew into Greek between 300 to 200 BC. The Greek word "lepra" meant nearly the same as tzaraat, and so the Greek translation used the term lepra. The word *tzaraat* has been translated to "leprosy" in many Bibles. King James Version Leviticus 13:3 gives the diagnosis: "…it is a plague of leprosy." The ESV (English Standard Version), BBE (Bible in basic English) and St. Joseph New Catholic Bible use the word leprosy. NIV (New International Version) uses the term "defiling skin disease"which is a better interpretation of the Hebrew.

### Diagnosis in the Old Testament

The ancient Israelites used a few ways to avoid improper diagnosis. One of the ways is still used by physicians today — simply wait and see if the rash disappears. The approach is described in Leviticus 13:

> *1 The LORD said to Moses and Aaron, 2 "When anyone has a swelling or a rash or a shiny spot on their skin that may be a **defiling skin disease**, they must be brought to Aaron the priest or to one of his sons who is a priest. 3 The priest is to examine the sore on the skin, and if the hair in the sore has turned white and the sore appears to be more than skin deep, it is a defiling skin disease. When the priest examines that person, he shall pronounce them*

*ceremonially unclean. 4 If the shiny spot on the skin is white but does not appear to be more than skin deep and the hair in it has not turned white, the **priest is to isolate the affected person for seven days**. 5 On the seventh day the priest is to examine them, and if he sees that the sore is unchanged and has not spread in the skin, he is to isolate them for another seven days. 6 On the seventh day the priest is to examine them again, and if the sore has faded and has not spread in the skin, the priest shall pronounce them clean; **it is only a rash**.*

Another way is to see if scabs formed. I guess that a rash all over the body and which a white scab formed would rule out small pox. Small pox was diagnosed in a 3000 year old Egyptian mummy, so we know that this disease existed in Biblical times. In Leviticus 13:

*[12] "If the disease breaks out all over their skin and, so far as the priest can see, it covers all the skin of the affected person from head to foot, [13] the priest is to examine them, and if the disease has covered their whole body, he shall pronounce them clean. Since it has all turned white, they are clean.*

But, if after a period of time there are open sores, the person is ruled as having *tzaraat,* and the person was considered to be unclean:

*14 But whenever raw flesh appears on them, they will be unclean. 15 When the priest sees the raw flesh, he shall pronounce them unclean. The raw flesh is unclean; they have a defiling disease.*

The diagnosis of a defiling skin disease led to shunning from the community for life. It was a harsh treatment. In Leviticus 13:

*45 "Anyone with such a defiling disease must wear torn clothes, let their hair be unkempt, cover the lower part of their face and cry out, 'Unclean! Unclean!' 46 As long as they have the disease they remain unclean. They must live alone; they must live outside the camp.*

**Jesus heals leprosy**

The New Testament, being originally written in Greek, uses the word "leprosy" from the Greek "lepra".

All three Synoptic Gospels of the New Testament describe an instance of Jesus healing a man with leprosy

(Matthew 8:1–4, Mark 1:40–45, and Luke 5:12–16). In Matthew 8:

> *1 When Jesus came down from the mountainside, large crowds followed him. 2 A man with leprosy came and knelt before him and said, "Lord, if you are willing, you can make me clean." 3 Jesus reached out his hand and touched the man. "I am willing," he said. "Be clean!" Immediately he was cleansed of his leprosy. 4 Then Jesus said to him, "See that you don't tell anyone. But go, show yourself to the priest and offer the gift Moses commanded, as a testimony to them."*

Note in the above story, Jesus tells the man who was healed to go to the religious authority to get verified that he was no longer unclean. The rules in Leviticus 13 and 14 were being followed. The gift Moses commanded in the above passage refers to Leviticus 14:4. This passage states that a leper when he was cured should give two live, clean birds, cedar-wood, scarlet, and hyssop.

Another instance of healing of leprosy is recorded in Luke 17:11–19. In this story, as Jesus was traveling, ten lepers called out to Jesus asking to be healed. Jesus told them to go to the priest to verify that they healed. Only one came back, a Samaritan, who threw himself at Jesus's feet, and thanked him for healing him. Jesus tells the man that his faith has healed him. Jesus remarks that a foreigner, a Samaritan, was the only one who was thankful. Since leprosy was such a serious disease, not to acknowledge thankfulness for being cured of leprosy would have been worse than rudeness.

**Leprosy in the Bible and now**

Two people are credited with discovering bacteria, and relating them to disease. Robert Koch (1843 – 1910) discovered the anthrax bacterium (*Bacillus anthracis*) in 1876, the date considered as the birth of modern bacteriology. He further discovered the causative agents of tuberculosis and cholera. His discoveries provided proofs for the germ theory of diseases, His contemporary, Louis Pasteur (1822 –1895), studied vaccination, microbial fermentation, and pasteurization.

Bacteria are killed by treatment with soap. During Colonial times, people made soap from tallow (fat of animals) and lye. After the Civil War, companies started making soap from other kinds of fat, such as palm oil or linseed oil. Soap became wide-spread in use. We teach our children to wash their hands with soap before eating, to reduce the possibility of bacterial and virus infection.  Soap has reduced bacteria skin diseases.

Leprosy is now known as Hansen's disease. It is named that in honor of Gerhard Armauer Hansen (1841 – 1912) who identified the bacteria causing the disease. Hansen's disease is the term often used by health care workers now, because the term leprosy remains so pejorative.

Bacteria are classified as being prokaryotes. They do not have a nucleus which are found in eukaryotes, such as amoeba and most cells in our body. Size of bacterium at 20- 400 nm is almost 1000 times smaller than the size of amoeba at 250-750 um. Bacteria are usually free-standing organisms; that is, they can live on their own provided that they have food.

Leprosy is caused by the specific bacteria *Mycobacterium leprae* or *Mycobacterium lepromatosis*. Leprosy bacteria affect skin, nerves and mucous membranes. They are not highly infectious and are not fast growing in the body. Scientists are unable to culture leprosy bacteria outside of the cell, and, isolated on a microscope slide, they live only a couple of hours. *M. leprae* invade peripheral nerves, especially, Schwann Cells. Schwann cells wrap around nerves and nerve roots and also produce the an insulation around nerve fibers called myelin. Without myelin nerves cannot transmit signals properly, hence impaired Schwann cells impairs nerve function. The leprosy bacterium prefers lower temperatures, so it invades cooler parts of the body — fingers, toes and nose.

Nerve damage underlies the gross pathology and deformity that are associated with leprosy. A symptom of leprosy is discolored patches of skin and thick, stiff or dry skin. When loss of sensation occurs, injuries such as burns may go unnoticed. Advanced leprosy can lead to paralysis and crippling, blindness and nose disfigurement.

**Was the skin disease of the Bible true leprosy (Hansen's disease)?**

The word "leprosy" used in many translations of the Old Testament most likely does not refer to true leprosy, Hansen's disease. Around 600 B.C. Indian writings describe a disease that resembles leprosy.

Leprosy causes changes in the skeleton. An Egyptian mummy from about 250 BC was identified as a leprosy sufferer. A skeleton from the first century AD was found in Israel that showed signs of leprosy. Evidence of leprosy in skeletal remains has not been found before that in this area.

So what happened around that time? Could have leprosy been spread from parts of Asia by the conquering armies? The army of Alexander the Great conquered India and known parts of Asia in about 326 BC. In Rome in 62 BC, coinciding with the return of Pompeii's troops from Asia Minor, there were reports of leprosy.

Although likely, we cannot be sure whether the disease of the New Testament was true leprosy. Definitive diagnosis in our times is identifying the bacterium causing the disease. Such a test was done for done on the remains of a people who were buried in the leper hospital at St Mary Magdalen in Winchester, UK. The remain are from 10th to 12th century burials. The genome sequences were very similar to the genomes of the bacterium *Mycobacterium leprae* from Sweden and the Middle East.

**Healing of leprosy in our day**

The first case of leprosy in the United States was reported in Louisiana in 1759 and in 1875 a case was reported in San Francisco. The largest leprosarium in United States was at Carville, Louisiana. In 1941, the director of the hospital there, Dr. Guy Foyt, discovered that sulfur drugs could cure the disease, and often reverse the symptoms. During this time it also became recognized that leprosy was not very contagious. A combination of medicines is now used to cure the infection. Gradually, fewer people were housed in leprosaria.

Leprosy is still wide spread around the world but the incidence of leprosy is decreasing, due to effective treatment. About 130,000 new leprosy cases in 139 countries were reported in 2020. The hope is that eventually no one will have leprosy. Will that mean leprosy will be eradicated? For humans, probably leprosy will never again be a feared infectious disease.

But leprosy has spread to animals. Leprosy occurs in the red squirrel found in the British Isles. And leprosy is found in nine-banded armadillos in Texas, USA and the state of Nuevo León, Mexico. Since leprosy was not found in the New World before Europeans invaded, the armadillos must have gotten it from humans who came from Europe. Armadillos are mammals, but they have cooler temperature than most other mammals. The bacterium *Mycobacterium leprae* grows best at lower temperatures, which is why extremities (nose, fingers, toes) are most affected in humans. Perhaps, the cooler temperature of armadillos made them a target for the bacterium.

## Leprosy in Hawaii

Sailors and settlers from Europe and America brought Hansen's disease to Hawaii. A Leprosarium in Molokai, Hawaii was established by King Kamehameha V in 1866. Anyone in Hawaii who got the disease was banished there, isolated from any contacts with their family. The primary landowner of the island, Molokai Ranch, was involved cattle ranching, pineapple and sugarcane production. The Molokai Ranch has now ceased operation. Unlike the rest of Hawaii islands, tourism is not developed on Molokai and then, and even now, the island is relatively scarcely populated. The leprosarium is located on a peninsula surrounded by rough ocean currents on one side and high cliffs on the other. People who were diagnosed with leprosy, were left off the side of the boat, and they swam through the high waves to the leper colony. They would never again have contact with their family. There was no internet, no telephone. Once there, their social isolation was complete.

Over 8000 people who were banished due to leprosy are buried at the site. The largest number of people there was in 1890, when 1100 people with leprosy lived there.

Since the 1940's Hansen's disease was curable. The leper colony operated until 1969. In 1980, the site was designated as Kalaupapa National Historical Park. People who had been inmates in the colony had been there many years in isolation. They lost contact with family and the rest of the world. Although cured of the disease, their bodies would have had disfigurement due to the disease. There are a few people who had suffered from leprosy still living there.

## Mold

Skin disease was greatly feared during Biblical times. In fact, even growths on surfaces of clothes, leather or houses were feared. Mildew is such growth. I suppose that mildew was considered "defiling skin disease of the house".

Houses get mold, and mold was considered equally dangerous as leprosy. Mildew required purification as detailed in Leviticus 14:33-57:

> [33] *The LORD said to Moses and Aaron,* [34] *"When you enter the land of Canaan, which I am giving you as your possession, and I put a spreading mildew in a house in that land,* [35] *the owner of the house must go and tell the priest, 'I have seen something that looks like mildew in my house.'* [36] *The priest is to order the house to be emptied before he goes in to examine the mildew, so that nothing*

*in the house will be pronounced unclean. After this the priest is to go in and inspect the house. [37] He is to examine the mildew on the walls, and if it has greenish or reddish depressions that appear to be deeper than the surface of the wall, [38] the priest shall go out the doorway of the house and close it up for seven days. [39] On the seventh day the priest shall return to inspect the house. If the mildew has spread on the walls, [40] he is to order that the* **contaminated stones be torn out and thrown** *into an unclean place outside the town.*

It seems drastic to us to tear down a house where mildew is found. Would we burn our house if our shower curtain got mildew? But the fear of leprosy was so great that destruction of the house is what was commanded. On the other hand, black mold still infects houses; it produces spores that cause allergic reactions. Black mold is a health risk, and you do not want it in your house.

After the mildew was eliminated as described in Leviticus, the house should be purified. Quite an elaborate purification ceremony was then done. It involved getting two birds, killing one, and dipping the live bird in the the blood of the dead bird, so that blood would be sprinkled throughout the house. The blood was mixed with hyssop and scarlet yarn.

Spreading of blood was atonement for the house (Leviticus 14; 40-57). Then, as now, the practice of medicine involves some hocus-pocus.

### Chapter 8

# Diseases of Nutrition

There are many diseases of nutrition. We are healthiest when we eat a variety of foods that contain vitamins, minerals and proteins. Many of the compounds that we eat are classified as micronutrients; we require them in very small quantities. I was interested that the supplement that is recommended for macular degeneration of the eye contains lutein and zeaxanthin. Both of these are carotenoids; they are related to the compounds that make carrots orange and tomatoes red. It follows, that eating red tomatoes and other vegetables will give these compounds to you.

The importance of vegetables was known to Daniel when he was residing in the court of Babylonian King Nebuchadnezzar (~642 BC- 562 BC) (Daniel 1). Daniel and his friends were chosen to be trained in the court for future royal service. They did not want to eat the rich food of the King's court. They insisted on nothing but vegetables to eat and water to drink. Within ten days they looked and felt better than the other trainees who were eating rich food and drinking wine.

This diet is now called "Daniel's diet" and you can find its use today as a way to lose weight and stay healthy. Micronutrients are important. But, overconsumption and underconsumption of food in general can be dangerous too. Diet can be misused and in this chapter I am writing about severe misuse of diet, in alcohol and food consumption.

## Alcoholism

Alcohol is a natural food. It forms when fruit decays, a result of actions of microbes. Birds, squirrels and humans that eat decaying apples, pumpkins, pears or other fruit can get drunk by ingesting fermented food. Fermentation of grapes leads to wine, of barley and grains to beer, and honey produces mead. During Bible times distillation to increase the alcohol content was probably not used. Distillation was first recorded in the 3rd century, about 200 years after Christ. Distillation of alcohol became prominent in Europe during the Middle Ages. The word "alcohol" comes from Arabic; the Arabs perfected distillation methods.

The amount of alcohol in fermented drinks is about 5 to 10%. Wine may go a bit higher than that. "Hard" liquor is distilled and alcohol content can be up to almost 100%. In spite of the fact that the drinks of the Bible were not as high in alcohol as distilled drinks, excessive consumption of naturally fermented drinks can lead to drunkenness and eventual alcoholism.

The formula for burning food was given in Chapter 2 on fire:

$$[\,C\,] + O_2 \longrightarrow CO_2 \text{ and } H_2O \quad \text{(Equation 1)}$$

When there is no $O_2$ present, some microorganisms break down sugar part way:

$$\text{sugar} \longrightarrow \text{alcohol} \quad \text{(Equation 2)}$$

Our bodies have two enzymes that change alcohol so it can be used for energy (or turned into fat). One enzyme takes it to another molecule (aldehyde) and the next enzyme takes it to an acid, acetic acid, a compound that contains 2 oxygen atoms. Acetic acid is vinegar. When wine gets sour, alcohol has turned to vinegar.  In our body, acetic acid ultimately gets broken down to $CO_2$ and $H_2O$ as in equation 1, or it is converted into fat. Some researchers think that the intermediate form of alcohol metabolism, aldehyde, is what is deleterious to the body.

Alcohol has given enjoyment to many, and, in moderation, its use over the entire time span of human existence shows that can be safe. But, it is dangerous in excess. In the immediate term, alcohol leads to drunkenness, impaired judgement, slow reaction response, lowered coordination and lowered concentration. It is estimated that 1/3 of traffic deaths in the United States have an alcohol involvement. More than 3 million accidents of criminal violence occurring annually in the US related to alcohol use. These physical violence incidences include aggression, rape, assault, child and spouse abuse, and homicide. In long term use, alcohol can lead to alcoholism. Many organs of the body are affected by long-time alcohol use. The liver becomes scarred, pancreas inflamed, arteries clogged, brain shrinks, heart contracts less strongly, kidney filters less well, kidney stones are more likely to form and blood pressure increases.

The overall health scenario is not good for excessive, long-term alcohol use. The Bible recognizes this many times. In Proverbs 20:1:

> *¹ Wine is a mocker and beer a brawler; whoever is led astray by them is not wise.*

Proverbs 23:29-35 describes the agony of someone who drinks too much wine:

> *²⁹ Who has woe? Who has sorrow? Who has strife? Who has complaints? Who has needless bruises? Who has*

*bloodshot eyes? [30] **Those who linger over wine**, who go to sample bowls of mixed wine. [31] Do not gaze at wine when it is red, when it sparkles in the cup, when it goes down smoothly! [32] In the end it bites like a snake and poisons like a viper. [33] Your eyes will see strange sights and your mind imagine confusing things. [34] You will be like one sleeping on the high seas, lying on top of the rigging. [35] "They hit me," you will say, "but I'm not hurt! They beat me, but I don't feel it! **When will I wake up so I can find another drink?**"*

In Galatians 5:19-21 drunkenness is equated with other sins:

*[19] The acts of the sinful nature are obvious: sexual immorality, impurity and debauchery; [20] idolatry and witchcraft; hatred, discord, jealousy, fits of rage, selfish ambition, dissensions, factions [21] and envy; **drunkenness**, orgies, and the like. I warn you, as I did before, that those who live like this will not inherit the kingdom of God.*

Paul, in 1 Corinthians 6, admonishes us to maintain a healthy life-style:

*[19] Do you not know that your body is a temple of the Holy Spirit, who is in you, whom you have received from God?*

*You are not your own; [20] you were bought at a price. Therefore honor God with your body.*

## The drunkenness of Noah and Lot

Drunkenness not only affects the drunk, but the whole family. Two stories in Genesis illustrate this.

In Genesis 9, Noah, after the flood, planted a vineyard and became drunk from wine. In drunken state he laid naked in his tent. It was forbidden to see your father or mother naked (Leviticus 18:6-20). Two of Noah's sons averted their eyes, but covered Noah. When Noah awakes, he curses Canaan, the child of Ham, the third of his sons. It seems strange that if Ham sinned against Noah, by not covering Noah, that his son Canaan was punished. There may be more to the story. But the story does illustrate the consternation and shame of Noah's drunkenness.

A shocking story concerning drunkenness of Lot, the nephew of Abraham, occurs in Genesis 19. Lot lives in Sodom, presumably as an influential person as he is at the gate of the city (Genesis 19:1). Two strangers visit Lot, and the men of the town clammer to have sex with the strangers. But Lot admonishes them for their wickedness, and offers the mob his two virgin daughters instead. Already, Lot seems sketchy to me, in that he does not protect his daughters. Lot knows that the people of Sodom are wicked and that God will destroy Sodom. Lot tries to bargain — if there are a minimum number of righteous people, would God save the city? But, no such people can be found, so Lot, his wife and two daughters run away as God rains brimstone on the Sodom and neighboring Gomorrah, and all the people perish. As they flee, Lot's wife looks back, she is turned into salt. Lot and his two daughters are now alone. They hide out in a cave. The daughters have lost their mother and their fiancés. They conspire to get Lot drunk and they have sex with their father in order to get pregnant. Their reasoning is that they want the family line to continue.

The picture is of a dysfunctional family who experienced great trauma. Some commentators say that it is likely that Lot raped his daughters, but the scriptures does not say that — the blame is put upon the daughters. In any case, Lot is complicit in that he accepted wine from his daughters, and he drank until he was drunk. The story is an example of loss of inhibitions due to alcohol consumption.

# Starvation

Through-out history many people have suffered from starvation. Withdrawing food has often been used as a tool to subjugate people. In the 1690's, perhaps about 15% of Scotland's population died in what is called the Seven Ill Years, and land reform displaced people from their crofts. The Irish Potato plague began in the middle of the 19th century, and it took the lives of an estimated 1 million people in Ireland. There was a political aspect of this famine in that the English government, either through neglect, apathy, or poor information, was blamed for not remedying the food shortage. In the Midwest of United States, European settlers deliberately killed the herds of bison, resulting in starvation of the Native Peoples. The war in Ukraine gives reminder of the history of Europe in the last century. In the 1930's an estimated 3.9 million people in Ukraine starved due to the harsh implement of collective farming imposed by the Russian dictator Joseph Stalin. This starvation event is called the Holodomor, and approximately one out of eight of Ukrainian population perished. During and immediately after the Second World war food shortages occurred over much of Europe. During the war, the situation in Greece was particularly grim. The country suffered from occupation by the Nazi's plus embargo by the Allied nations. Examples of starvation can be found in the history of peoples on every continent.

Sadly, hunger still exists on our planet. Hunger can mean lack or calories, or lack of essential foods or a combination of both. Many children of the world do not have enough protein in the diet. In extreme case, this diseases called Kwashiorkor. We continue to have over-population, wars, climate changes, evil or inept politicians and diseases. In 2019, the United Nations estimated that 690 million people world-wide were undernourished. In 2019, a little over 20% of all children in the world showed stunted growth, a result of not enough food. Starvation and malnutrition is the most prevalent disease in the world.

**Composition of food**

From a biochemical point of view what happens during starvation? Starvation is not just feeling a bit hungry at noon when you skipped breakfast. Major changes in metabolism occurs. There are three major food stuffs — fat, protein and carbohydrates. Here are their compositions:

**Carbohydrates** are made up of sugars.

**Proteins** are made up of amino acids.

**Fat** is made up mainly of two carbon units. (The simplest 2 C food is acetic acid. It is contained in vinegar).

Proteins do things — they make up our connective tissue, enzymes, and molecules that carry out the chores of the cell. They do the work. Carbohydrates and fat are storage molecules that are ultimately used for energy. The storage form of carbohydrates is called glycogen. Glycogen is broken down to sugar for "quick energy". The analogous compound in plants provide us with flour or starch. Fat is used for energy and it is stored in fat, ie. adipose, tissue. Fat is transported in the blood as triglyceride and fatty acids. These names may be familiar to you from blood levels of these compounds allows physicians to evaluate your health. When you eat in excess, whether you eat fat, protein or carbohydrate, these compounds get converted into fat, and then stored in fat tissue.

A satisfying diet contains a mixture of carbohydrates, proteins and fat. The Bible records an instance when we can conjecture excess carbohydrate was eaten. In Exodus 16 the Israelites were experiencing harsh conditions in the desert as they made their way to the Promised Land.   They find a white substance, called manna, which they equate with bread (a carbohydrate) that they say tasted like wafers made with honey. So manna was sweet. To this day, an insect (*Trabutina manniparain*) in the Sinai  and Arabian deserts secrete a sweet nectar.  These insects feed on tamarack bushes which are native to the area. This nectar dries and forms a white, flaky substance. .The Bedouins that still live in these deserts use this substance to sweeten tea, just as we use honey, also made from an insect. The secretion from manna insects contains a mixture of sugars. Pure types of sugars, such as sucrose which is table sugar, melt or decompose at a high temperature. A mixture of various sugars melts at a lower temperature — think of corn syrup or maple syrup. The Bible records that manna melted when the sun became hot (Exodus 16:21). Also, manna did not keep well: keeping it overnight attracted maggots and the manna began to smell (Exodus 16: 19-20).  Flies are attracted to sweet things. The properties of manna described in the Bible would all be consistent with it being composed of sugars.

The Israelites's diet was supplemented by eating birds, but they still complained about all that manna. In Numbers 11 they remember eating meat and vegetables back in Egypt:

*⁴The rabble with them began to crave other food, and again the Israelites started wailing and said, "If only we had meat to eat! [5] We remember the fish we ate in Egypt at no cost—also the cucumbers, melons, leeks, onions and garlic. [6] But now we have lost our appetite; we never see anything but this manna!"*

Manna was likely similar to our candy. If we were eating candy all the time, we would probably also be whining for cucumbers, melons and onions. Food also has a psychological effect. We like the foods of our childhood. The Israelites remembered the food that they used to eat.

**Starvation effects on the body**

To put it in simple terms, when we eat more food than what we expend, fat is made as follows (where —> means "converted to" ):

protein —> fat;

sugar —> fat;

fat —> fat.

These equations basically say that when we eat more than what we use for energy, we get fat.

When we are not eating:

glycogen —> sugar

protein —> sugar

fat —> 2 carbon compound (acetic acid)

Fat <u>cannot be converted into protein</u> and fat cannot be <u>converted into sugar</u>. Our bodies do not have the enzymes to do so.

And here is another thing to know. The **brain** uses sugar (from carbohydrate in diet and from glucose from the stored form of sugar, glycogen) as a fuel. Unlike most tissues the brain does not use fat for energy.  As note above, fat cannot be made into sugar.

So, what happens during starvation? The body uses fat to allow our heart to beat and us to move. But, what about the brain? It cannot use fat. The body protects the brain to keep it alive. Initially, fat is used up by most tissues, whereas the brain uses sugar that it gets from glycogen that is stored in the liver, and glucose released into the blood stream.  Without eating for 10 or more hours, glycogen in liver is used up, and protein will start to be broken down to make sugar to keep the brain alive. Even as you sleep overnight protein begins to be broken down, being made into glucose for the brain to consume. This is why it is recommended to eat breakfast. Glycogen is also used up during strenuous exercise, and then protein is also broken down. Athletic trainers recommend a protein drink after prolonged, strenuous exercise. Supplying amino acids from a protein drink

132

allows the body to rebuild muscle which is mainly made up of proteins

Long term fasting is more dangerous. When glycogen from liver is used up, the body starts to break down protein to make sugar to keep the brain alive. In long term starvation, other chemicals, called ketones, are made from fat and these compounds are also used by the brain. But the longer a person is deprived of food, the more protein is broken down. Muscle is mainly made from protein. Therefore, during starvation muscle is lost and the person becomes weak. Antibodies, which protect us against viruses and bacteria, are made of protein. During starvation, level of antibodies decrease, and immunity from disease decreases. Bones and joints are held together with protein; starvation leads to painful joints and brittle bones. Proteins are used in the intestines to transport nutrients, and absorption of food is impaired. The level of electrolytes in blood and cells are regulated by proteins of the intestine, as well as kidneys. Loss of proper levels of electrolytes can lead to heart problems, dizziness, weakness, cognitive impairment and muscle cramps. Studies of people who were starving during World War II reveal that there are long term effects on the heart, especially when starvation occurred during puberty.

A sad case of starvation occurred with the death of singer Karen Carpenter in 1983. She suffered from an eating disorder, probably *anorexia nervosa*, a condition where the person voluntarily does not eat. Her death was ruled as heart failure. The heart is a muscle, and muscles are composed of protein; during food deprivation muscle is lost as the amino acids of protein are converted into sugar to keep the brain functioning. After a long time of starvation, the heart was not strong enough to keep pumping blood.

**Food is equated with love**

Carl, one of my brothers, recounts a story that happened when he was 5 or 6. We were living in Amherst, South Dakota and he accompanied our Dad on a drive for some errand and a ground blizzard occurred. The driving conditions were very bad and temperature was dropping. He and Dad were very relieved when they finally made it home. The house was warm and Mother was baking bread. He says to him that heaven will have the smell of fresh made bread and the warmth and comfort of home and loved ones.

Jesus recognizes the love of parents to their children when he says in Matthew 7:7-10:

When your child, whom you love, is hungry you feed
him.

### Hunger in the Bible

Starvation is a painful, long-term and ultimately lethal
disease. It is much more than craving for a chocolate bar, say.
Hunger of starvation affects every organ in the entire body.
When we realize the severity of starvation, passages about
hunger in the Bible have more meaning.  Throughout both the
Old and New Testament, hunger is equated with a desire to
know God.

Famine is central to the story of the Israelites, and the
plays a role in the story of Joseph in Egypt. Due to jealously
from his brother, the brothers sold Joseph into slavery in Egypt.
While in Egypt, he rose to a position of high rank. During that
time Pharaoh had dreams, which Joseph interpreted as
predicting times of good harvests and times of famine. Not only
was Joseph prescient in predicting the future, he also had an
idea how to save people from the dangers of famine. He

organized the storage of grain to tide people over during famine. It was then that his brothers went to Egypt to get food.

### Spiritual food

A constant theme is that God will care for us. When the Israelites were about to enter the Promised Land, Moses gave sermons to them on the plains of Moab, and reminds them how the Lord cared for them. In Deuteronomy 8:3, Moses says:

> *3 He humbled you, causing you to hunger and then **feeding** you with manna, which neither you nor your fathers had known, to teach you that **man does not live on bread alone** but on every word that comes from the mouth of the LORD.*

Just as we need physical food, we need spiritual food.

The devil attempts to use hunger to manipulate Jesus when Jesus was in the desert. Matthew 4:1-25 recounts:

> *1 Then Jesus was led by the Spirit into the desert to be tempted by the devil. 2 After fasting forty days and forty nights, he was hungry. 3 The tempter came to him and said, "If you are the Son of God, tell these stones to become bread." 4 Jesus answered, "It is written: '**Man does not live***

*on bread alone, but on every word that comes from the mouth of God.'"*

Note that Jesus quotes Deuteronomy 8:3 verbatim in answering the devil. We definitely need food, but we need more than that. We need the word of God.

**Being fed**

The verses below about being fed after being hungry are some of the most evocative in the Bible.

John 6:35 states:

³⁵ Then Jesus declared, **"I am the bread of life**. He who comes to me will never go hungry, and he who believes in me will never be thirsty.

Matthew 5:1-12, is from the Sermon on the Mont:

*¹ Now when he saw the crowds, he went up on a mountainside and sat down. His disciples came to him, ² and he began to teach them saying: ³ "Blessed are the poor in spirit, for theirs is the kingdom of heaven. ⁴ Blessed are those who mourn, for they will be comforted. ⁵ Blessed are the meek, for they will inherit the earth. ⁶**Blessed are those who hunger and thirst for righteousness, for they will be filled**.*

137

### Helping others

Along with the analogy of physical and spiritual hunger, the Bible writers are constant in their admonition that we should help others who are hungry. The implication is that the experience of not having food makes us empathetic to others. The knowledge that God gives us spiritual food, should make us want to help with the physical food of others. Giving to others is equivalent to giving to Jesus, as in Matthew 25:35:

> *35 For I was hungry and you gave me something to eat, I was thirsty and you gave me something to drink, I was a stranger and you invited me in,*

Many verses of the Bible tell us to share our bounties with others. The verse from the prophet Isaiah (Isaiah 58:10) states:

> *10 and if you spend yourselves in behalf of the hungry and satisfy the needs of the oppressed, then your light will rise in the darkness, and your night will become like the noonday.*

In James 2:15-17 food and clothes should be shared:

> *15 Suppose a brother or sister is without clothes and daily food. 16 If one of you says to him, "Go, I wish you well;*

*keep warm and well fed," but does nothing about his physical needs, what good is it? ¹⁷ In the same way, faith by itself, if it is not accompanied by action, is dead.*

The over-arching message of the Bible is that we will never suffer want in Jesus. Both food and water will be given to us. The passage In Revelation 7:16-17 is comforting to us:

*¹⁶ **Never again will they hunger;** never again will they thirst. The sun will not beat upon them, nor any scorching heat. ¹⁷ For the Lamb at the center of the throne will be their shepherd; he will lead them to springs of living water. And God will wipe away every tear from their eyes."*

## Obesity

An epidemiologist friend once told me that half of the world over-eats and the other half does not have enough food. He said that if we could take food from the over-eaters and give it to the famished, everyone in the world would be in better health.

The Bible equates over-eating with over-imbibing of alcohol. In Proverbs 23: 20-21:

*[20] Do not join those who drink too much wine or gorge themselves on meat, [21] for **drunkards** and **gluttons** become poor, and drowsiness clothes them in rags.*

## Obesity in history and in the Bible

In history there are not as many instances of obesity as compared to starvation. This is because for most of history, food was not plentiful. But, ancient people did know about obesity, even during prehistoric times. Neolithic "Venus" figures are small stone carvings of anatomically-correct obese women found throughout Eurasia (Google "The Venus of Willendorf" to see a picture). These carvings date from perhaps 35,000 to 40,000 years ago. For people living on the edge of starvation, obesity would have been considered a sign of health and beauty. Fat is the way the body stores energy for times when food is scarce.

At the Museum of Modern Judaism in Casablanca, Morocco I saw wedding dresses for Jewish brides that were several hundred years old. It was apparent that stout, short women wore these dresses. The Jewish community had the custom that the bride-to-be would be fattened up before her wedding. This custom makes sense because she soon would be pregnant and she would be able to nourish a developing baby even if food was scarce. In the Book of Esther (Esther 2,12), it is recalled that Esther underwent twelve months of beauty treatments before she was brought to the King. This would also probably involved eating rich foods.

A graphic Bible story about obesity is Ehud's story, found in Judges 3:12-30. At that time the Israelites were being ruled by an evil king, a Moabite by name of Eglon. I quote the whole story because the Bible narrative is so clear about what happened:

*15 Again the Israelites cried out to the Lord, and he gave them a deliverer—Ehud, a left-handed man.... The Israelites sent him with tribute to Eglon king of Moab. 16 Now Ehud had made a double-edged sword about a cubit long, which he strapped to his right thigh under his clothing. 17 He presented the tribute to Eglon king of Moab, who was a very fat man. 18 After Ehud had presented the tribute, he sent on their way those who had carried it. 19 But on reaching the stone images near Gilgal he himself went back to Eglon and said, "Your Majesty, I have a secret message for you."*

*The king said to his attendants, "Leave us!" And they all left.*

*[20] Ehud then approached him while he was sitting alone in the upper room of his palace and said, "I have a message from God for you." As the king rose from his seat, [21] Ehud reached with his left hand, drew the sword from his right thigh and plunged it into the king's belly. [22] Even the handle sank in after the blade, and his bowels discharged. Ehud did not pull the sword out, and the fat closed in over it. [23] Then Ehud went out to the porch; he shut the doors of the upper room behind him and locked them.*

*[24] After he had gone, the servants came and found the doors of the upper room locked. They said, "He must be relieving himself in the inner room of the palace." [25] They waited to the point of embarrassment, but when he did not open the doors of the room, they took a key and unlocked them. There they saw their lord fallen to the floor, dead. [26] While they waited, Ehud got away...*

As a mystery story, this story rivals anything on the Columbo TV show or books written by Agatha Christie. Mystery fiction writers emphasize that criminal suspects must have <u>motive</u>, <u>means</u>, and <u>opportunity</u>.

Did Ehud have motive? Yes, Eglon was a bad king.

Did he have means? Yes. First he made the sword, showing premeditation. And he took advantage of the fact that he was left-handed. Because he was left-handed, his drawing of the sword (from his left side to the sword on his right) and the direction of his stabbing would be unexpected.

Did Ehud have opportunity? Yes, he got access to King Eglon by giving him tribute. Then he pretended that he had a secret to tell him. And after the stabbing, because Eglon was so fat, he could leave the sword inside him — no need to be caught with a bloody sword when he ran out. If no autopsy was done, perhaps the murder weapon would not even have been found!

Finally, he was able to make his escape because Eglon's servants thought he was using the toilet. Constipation would be common for someone who does not exercise and who eats too much, especially not eating fruits, vegetables or fiber!

Ehud used a sword one cubit long. A cubit had two definitions at this time. One definition made it about 45 cm (18 inches) and the other made it 52 cm (20 inches). Taking the shorter definition of 18 inches, Eglon would have had to be very fat. The fattest people recorded now living weigh up to 1000 pounds. If the lean weight of such a person is 150 pounds, their body would be 85% fat. A very rough estimate (by me) is that Eglon could have weighed up to 600 pounds.

### Chapter 9

# Dates and Palms

The Bible spans a very long time.  Abraham, the father of Judaism, Christianity and Islam, lived perhaps at 2200-2100 BCE.  The last book of the Bible is Revelations, attributed to John the Elder was written in about 90 - 100 AD.  Abraham was a nomad; he herded sheep. Cheese had already been used for food since about 5000 BCE; wine. also has an ancient history. Wheat and barley had been domesticated by then. But chariots drawn by horses came later. Domesticated camels came to Israel by 930 BCE. By 100 AD, many animals and plants had been domesticated and there were trade routes to transport food from one place to another. The diet of people living during the Roman times would have reflected their cosmopolitan society. Food found in jars of Roman shipwrecks show that olive oil, wheat, dates, and dried fish were transported from one area to another in Jesus' times.

We would have been comfortable eating the foods that were served during Jesus's time. But, we would not have been able to celebrate a traditional United States Thanksgiving dinner. Turkey, cranberries, potatoes, sweet potatoes, wild rice and tomatoes are all New World foods. We would not have been able to have pumpkin pie or pecan pie for dessert. Corn is mentioned many times in the Bible, but it would not have been corn plant as we Americans call it. When we eat "corn on the cob" we are eating the plant with the botanical name *Zea mays*. The rest of world uses the common name maize for this plant. Corn in the Bible means any type of grain. Types of bean grown in Biblical times include lentils, chickpeas and fava beans. Fava beans cause red blood cells to break open in people who have an enzyme variant often found in some people in the Mediterranean region. Pythagoras (580–500 BCE) warns about this, so we know fava beans was common in the diet at that time. Lima and kidney beans came from the New World.

I am writing this on the week before Palm Sunday. Because of this, rather than writing about many plants and animals in the Bible, I am going to focus on date palms. Palm Sunday occurs on the Sunday before Easter. It commemorates

Jesus' triumphal entry into Jerusalem, when people waved palms as he rode a donkey into Jerusalem. In John 12:

> *13 They took **palm branches** and went out to meet him, shouting,*
>
> *"Hosanna!"*
>
> *"Blessed is he who comes in the name of the Lord!"*
>
> *"Blessed is the king of Israel!"*

### Palm trees

Around 2,600 species of palms are known of the family *Arecaceae*. Palms grow in tropic and subtropic areas. If an area is cool without temperatures going below freezing palms can grow there, too. I was surprised to see palm trees growing in Bristol, England (latitude further north than Winnipeg, Canada) and in western Scotland. This area is warmed by the Gulf current.

Palms produce edible fruits that are consumed today, such as coconut, date, and acai berry. Fruits from other palm trees species are eaten locally. Heart of palm is a white vegetable obtained from the center of specific varieties of palm tree. Leaves of palms are used for shelter and building material.

Oil from coconuts is used in many cuisines, especially in southeast Asia. Coconut flour is sometimes used as a substitute for wheat flour by people with wheat gluten intolerance.

### Date palms

Dates are mentioned more than 50 times in the Bible. Date palms are beautiful trees. The Hebrew word for the date palm is 'tamar'. "Tamar" is used as a woman's name and It means grace and elegance. King David's beautiful daughter was named Tamar (2 Samuel 13). Song of Solomon 7:7 uses a palm tree to describe the beauty of a woman:

*"Your stature is like a palm tree,*

*And your breasts are like its clusters.*

Palm trees are used as symbols of prosperity. In Psalm 92 :

*[12] The righteous will flourish like a palm tree  they will grow like a cedar of Lebanon;*

*[13] planted in the house of the Lord,  they will flourish in the courts of our God.*

Palm trees were so highly regarded that Solomon used them to decorate his temple, made in 957 BCE. In 1 Kings 6:31-33 Solomon's building is described:

*So he made two doors of olive wood, and he carved on them carvings of cherubim, palm trees, and open flowers, and overlaid them with gold; and he spread the gold on the cherubim and on the palm trees.*

Solomon's temple was destroyed, but palms were also used to decorate the Second Temple. Ezekiel 40:16 records the prophet's view of the restored temple:

*⁶The alcoves and the projecting walls inside the gateway were surmounted by narrow parapet openings all around, as was the portico; the openings all around faced inward. The faces of the projecting walls were **decorated with palm trees**.*

### Palm branches in celebration

Palm branches are used through-out the Mesopotamian and Mediterranean world. Both ancient Greek and Rome used palm branches to wave at war heroes as they paraded through the streets following successful battles. The branches were a symbol of victory and triumph.

The idea of palm branches to symbolize victory was used by John the Elder in Revelation 7:9:

*⁹ After this I looked, and there before me was a great multitude that no one could count, from every nation, tribe, people and language, standing before the throne and before the Lamb. They were wearing white robes and were holding **palm branches** in their hands.*

In this case, the palm branches symbolized victory over sin.

**Dates as food**

We consider the dietary benefits of dates. On average, dates contain 21% water, 75% carbohydrates (63% sugar and 8% fiber, 2% protein, and less than 1 % fat. So, the primary nutrient of dates is sugar. Dates also contain pantothenic acid, vitamin B6 and minerals including magnesium, manganese, and potassium.

There are many types of sugars, but the most common in our diet are these three: sucrose, glucose and fructose. Most fruits and vegetables contain a mixture of these three sugars. Glucose is the type of sugar that is circulating in our blood. It is the sugar required by our brain and used in other organs for energy. Fructose from the diet is transported from the stomach and intestine directly to the liver. The liver converts fructose to glucose and this glucose is put into the blood stream or stored in the liver as glycogen. Glucose and fructose are classified as simple sugars (they are made up of 6 carbon atoms). Sucrose is the sugar in our sugar bowl that we put on cereal and in coffee. Sucrose is more complicated: It is composed of two simple sugar units. It is called a disaccharide, and it is made up form one part glucose and one part fructose sugar groups. To make sucrose available as fuel to tissues, including brain, the sucrose molecule must be cut in halt to yield glucose and fructose. Fructose is then converted to glucose, and glucose is then available as fuel for the body.

Of the sugar in dates, 55% is fructose and 45% is glucose. In comparison, an orange has 51%sucrose, 26% fructose and 23% glucose. An apple has 17% sucrose, 62% fructose and 20% glucose. Because the body needs to convert fructose and sucrose into glucose which takes some time, eating glucose directly will cause blood sugar to rise faster than eating sucrose and fructose. People who are prone to sudden drops in blood sugar, such as some diabetics, are prescribed pure glucose tablets. Dates are a good source of "quick energy" because of their high glucose content. They are also less expensive than glucose tablets and taste good!

I mentioned before my trip to Morocco. One highlight of the trip was riding a camel in the Sahara desert. After the ride, our tour guide served us tea with mint and dates. Tea and dates were a great pick-me-up after the hot, dry camel ride.

Israeli date honey is a syrup made from dates. In Exodus 3:17 the Israelites were promised a land filled with "milk and honey". Some scholars believe that "honey" refers to date honey, not honey from bees. Date honey is available for purchase on-line, and I imagine it can be used in cooking like how corn syrup and honey are used.

### Judean date palm

The area of Palestine was a big date-producing area during Biblical times. In Deuteronomy 34:3, Moses was shown the Promised Land and Jericho was called the "city of palm trees".

The Judean date palm was exported to Rome during Jesus's times. This particular variety of date was renowned for its sweetness. It also kept better than other dates, presumably because it had a lower water content. Bacteria that cause food spoilage require water, which is why dry foods last longer than moist foods.

The Judean date palm is documented in archeological and written documents. Unfortunately, in about year 1000 AD this variety became extinct. If the editor of the book would allow it, here is where I would place a sad emoji.

Why did it go extinct? What happened in about 1000 AD? This was the time of the Crusades, but scholars think it is unlikely that the Crusaders would have caused the extinction of the tree. It was also a time of climate cooling. A cooler climate could have made it impossible for the date tree to pollinate.

So, does that mean that we will never taste the date variety that Jesus and the disciples ate? There is more to the story. In 1963, archeologists excavated the fortress at Masada, built by King Herod the Great. They found some dates in a jar, and carbon-dated them to originate from between 156 BCE and 64 CE. Therefore, these dates came from about the time of Christ. The date seed were stored in a museum for 40 years, when Dr. Sarah Sallon (from Sustainable Agriculture at the Arava Institute for Environmental Research) got the idea to try to grow trees from them. Three seeds were planted and one seed germinated and grew.

Here is where I should put a smiling emoji. But, not so fast. Palm trees, like many other trees including white as (*Fraxinus americana*), ginkgo (*Ginkgo biloba*), boxelder (*Acer negundo*) and holly (*Ilex aquifolim*), have male and female flowers on separate individuals. In order to get fruit, the pollen from a male tree needs to pollinate the flower from a female tree. The tree that germinated from the 2000 year old seed was male. He was named Methuselah. no fruit would be coming from Methuselah (sad emoji). However, the researcher mated his pollen with another palm tree variety, and dates were produced. The genes in these dates are one-half Judean palm.

The story continues, though. Additional seeds from ancient times were found in Qumran, the site where the Dead Sea Scrolls were found. Some of these seeds also sprouted and grew into plants. One of these plants was named Hannah. Hannah began to make fruit when pollenated by Methuselah. These fruit are 100% Judean palm. Someday when more trees are planted, we might be able to taste dates from them.

Methuselah was grown from the oldest seed ever documented. Methuselah has an interesting characteristic in that it has thorns. Plants that grow in areas where there are no animals that eat them usually do not have thorns nor are they poisonous. In instance, the native plants of Hawaii, where there were no large herbivores, produce no example of poisonous fruit or thorny branches. The ancestors of Methuselah grew in an area of sheep and goats. Thorns would have been protection from being eaten.

Jesus had a crown of thorns placed upon him during his crucifixion. It is possible that palm trees provided branches to praise him during his triumphal entry into Jerusalem, also provided the thorns at his death.

Chapter 10

# Vision: A metaphor for our times

### Eyes: How do we see?

We can sense hot/cold, touch, sound, taste, smell and light. Of these senses, our ability to sense light is the best understood. My research involved the use of light to study proteins. Consequently, for me, the most interesting sense that we have is vision.

In this essay, we are going to think about how people viewed vision over the ages, how the Bible views vision, give an example where a scientific theory gave rise to a superstition, and, finally, an example where we see correctly but interpret incorrectly.

156

**Vision theories**

Ancient Greeks gave us the first theories of vision. One, pioneered by the mathematician Euclid (about 300 BCE), hypothesized that vision required rays coming from our eyes. Plato (428 BCE–328 BCE) and his followers also advocated that light consisted of rays emitted by the eyes. The second theory current at around the same time, said that something entered the eye that resembled the object that you are seeing. Aristotle (384-322 BCE) and Democritus (460 BC–370 BCE) believed that the visual image did not arise directly in the eye, but the air between the object and the eye is contacted and stamped by the seen object and the observing eye.

Ibn al-Haytham (aka. Alhazen, 965 – c. 1040 AD) was the first to explain that vision occurs when light reflects from an object and then passes to one's eyes. He thus paved the way for the study of optics. He was also the first to demonstrate that vision occurs in the brain, rather than in the eyes. Issac Newton (1642-1726) showed that white light can be separated into colors when passing through a prism. Christiaan Huygens (1629-1695) and Newton proposed competing theories for light's behavior. Huygens proposed a wave theory of light while Newton's was a "corpuscular" (particle) theory of light. Our thinking about light is a combination of Huygens and Newton's theories — under some conditions light appears to be corpuscular and other conditions as a wave.

We know now when light hits an object, some of the light is absorbed by that object. The rest of the light is scattered or transmitted through the object. When scattered light hits our eye, the light beam is focused by the lens onto a membrane called the retina. Retina contains a protein called rhodopsin. The rhodopsin protein binds a molecule, called retinol, which chemically changes when light hits it. This causes a neuronal signal to go from the specialized cells containing rhodopsin to the brain and the brain interprets the light that impinged upon the eye as vision. There are two kinds of cells that detect light: rods and cones. Rods detect low levels of light, and we see only black and white in dim light. Bright light activates the cones allowing us to see colors.

**Eyes In the Bible**

The Bible generally implies that the eye is not a passive organ, receiving light. Jesus seems to be subscribing to the Euclidian theory when he says in Matthew 6:22:

*"The **eye is the lamp of the body**. If your eyes are healthy, your whole body will be full of light. 23 But if your eyes are unhealthy, your whole body will be full of darkness. If then the light within you is darkness, how great is that darkness!*

The eye needs to be actively involved in vision as expressed in Psalm 115:5:

*They have mouths, but they cannot speak;*

*They have eyes, but they cannot see;*

John 12 records the last part of Jesus' ministry.  In John 12 34-36 Jesus is equates light with himself.  Seeing is equal to believing.

*³⁴ The crowd spoke up, "We have heard from the Law that the Messiah will remain forever, so how can you say, 'The Son of Man must be lifted up'? Who is this 'Son of Man'?"*

*³⁵ Then Jesus told them, "You are going to have the **light** just a little while longer. Walk while you have the light, before **darkness** overtakes you. Whoever walks in the dark does not know where they are going. **36** Believe in the light while you have the light, so that you may become children of light."*

The passage goes on stating that the people of Israel continued not to believe him. Jesus quotes the prophet Isaiah this foretelling this in John 12-39-40:

*39......, as Isaiah says elsewhere:*

*40 "He has blinded their eyes and hardened their hearts so they can neither see with their eyes nor understand with their hearts nor turn—and I would heal them."*

It is clear in the Bible is that eye and understanding go hand-in-hand. Even today, when we say "I see" it means "I understand" or "I believe".

A passage from Numbers 6 gives us a Benediction, the words used at the end of a church service.  These are word the Lord said to Moses to tell Aaron to use as a blessing to the Israelites.

24 "The Lord bless you and keep you;

25 **the Lord make his face shine on you** and be gracious to you;

26 the Lord **turn his face toward you** and give you peace."

I think that the high-lighted lines are of the most beautiful and evocative passages in the Bible. God, by looking at you, blesses and keeps you, and He gives you peace. The passage gains more meaning when we realize that the ancient people's theory of vision is that there are rays coming from the eyes. God, by facing us, is actively working for us.

### Mirror reflection

Most things scatter light in a random fashion. But, mirrored surfaces reflect the light such that you see an image. If we subscribe to the Euclidean theory of vision, one can ask what happens to vision when it is reflected. In Greek mythology, when a man looked at the goddess Medusa, he would turn to stone. But, the emitted rays from Medusa was not reflected in the mirror. Because of this, Perseus was able to slay the evil Medusa while looking at the reflection from the mirrored shield he received from Athena

I imagine that Paul was thinking of this effect of mirrors when he wrote in 1 Corinthians 13:12:

*For now we see only a reflection as in a mirror; then we shall see face to face. Now I know in part; then I shall know fully, even as I am fully known.*

When we know the background of the theory of vision, we can surmise that Paul is saying that now we cannot fully understand God. We do not see the whole thing when we look in a mirror.  But, just as God fully understand us, in the future we will be able to comprehend God's love.

### Evil eye

Our view of vision is not exactly like either of the ancient Greek theories. But these theories from more than 2000 years ago remain in popular psyche and superstition. The theory of Euclid gives rise to concept of Evil Eye, the idea that a malevolent, surreptitious look from someone can cause evil to you.

That the eye can cause harm or change personality is expressed in Proverbs 28:2:

*A man with an evil eye hastens after wealth*
*And does not know that want will come upon him.*

I was surprised to find how much jewelry with an evil eye you can find on-line. The idea of wearing evil-eye jewelry is that if someone casts an evil eye on you, then the amulet will reflect it back on that person. You will not be injured. Perhaps, some people wear this jewelry solely as a fashion statement and not as an amulet. I was surprised to find an "evil-eye" piece in my jewelry collection. It had been a gift, and I had no idea what it meant until I researched this chapter.

### How do we see colors?

I have a plant in the window of the room where I am. I see the plant as being green. That means that the plant absorbs all colors of light except green. Green is scattered to my eye. So, another way to look at it, is that the plant is all colors, except green.  There is always more than one way to understand things.

So, how does the eye see colors? We have three color receptors in retina of our eye which allows us to see the colors displayed in the spectrum. This depiction of the colors of light is called the electromagnetic spectrum. Babies and children can see below 400 nm, into what we call the ultraviolet range. Cataracts that form in old age block out some of the blue region of the spectrum. After cataract surgery, people are often surprised how blue the sky is; they had been seeing less and less blue while the cataract developed.

We see the spectrum as being composed as distinct colors. But there is a continual distribution of wavelengths. In my lab, I had instrumentation that would distinguish 500.01 nm light from 500.02 nm light. Even better instruments exists in other labs. My eye would see these two colors as the same — green.  To see color, we need light — electromagnetic radiation

163

— and a detector in the eye. Our eyes have three color detectors (called receptors), and when we see a given color we are seeing actually seeing a wide swatch of wavelengths.

To give you an idea of the size of a wavelength of light, we can compare with the size of cells in our body. Human red blood cells are about 8 um, or $8 \times 10^{-6}$ meters in diameter. Blue light is 400 nm or $0.4 \times 10^{-6}$ meters long. Therefore, the cell is about 20 times longer than the wavelength of light.

### Colors in the Bible

Joseph and his "Amazing Technicolor Coat" probably comes to mind when you think about colors in the Bible. Many colors are mentioned in the Bible. In researching this chapter, I found that indigo dye, made from the indigo plant, originated in Indus Valley and was used in Mesopotamia by the 7th Century BC. Blue dye was also obtained from an shellfish, so either the animal dye or indigo dye was probably used to give blue color In Exodus 26:36:

> *"You shall make a screen for the entrance of the tent, of blue and purple and scarlet yarns and fine twined linen, embroidered with needlework.*

Indigo plant was introduced to South Carolina from Africa by slaves. The dye was used by Levi Strauss to make iconic blue jeans during the California gold rush. The "Blue Men of the Sahara" — Bedouin nomads — wear indigo dyed clothes to this day.

The book of Revelation uses most symbolism of color in the Bible. The apostle John, author of the book especially uses colored stones for symbols. Here is an example Revelation 4 with stones and colors highlighted by bold font:

*After this I looked, and there before me was a door standing open in heaven. And the voice I had first heard speaking to me like a trumpet said, "Come up here, and I will show you what must take place after this." 2 At once I was in the Spirit, and there before me was a throne in heaven with someone sitting on it. 3 And the one who sat there had the appearance of **jasper** and **ruby**. A **rainbow** that shone like an **emerald** encircled the throne. 4Surrounding the throne were twenty-four other thrones, and seated on them were twenty-four elders. They were dressed in **white** and had crowns of **gold** on their heads.*

In Revelation 21 the New City in the Kingdom of God is described:

*[18] The wall was made of jasper, and the city of pure gold, as pure as glass. [19] The foundations of the city walls were decorated with every kind of precious stone. The first foundation was **jasper**, the second **sapphire**, the third **agate**, the fourth **emerald**, 20 the fifth **onyx**, the sixth **ruby**, the seventh **chrysolite**, the eighth **beryl**, the ninth **topaz**, the tenth **turquoise**, the eleventh **jacinth**, and the twelfth **amethyst**. 21 The twelve gates were twelve **pearls**, each gate made of a single pearl. The great street of the city was of **gold**, as pure as transparent glass.*

The twelve gem stones harken back to the breastplate of Aaron, brother of Moses, in Exodus, 28:15-30. In the case of Aaron, the twelve stones refer to the twelve tribes of Israel. In Revelations, John uses beautiful colored gem stones to illustrate the beauty of the future New Heaven and New Earth.

**Race in the Bible**

Sadly, color has come to mean race in our country. This is an example where we see correctly, but interpret incorrectly.

Look at the colors around you. Do you know people who are deep blue, bright red, green or yellow? In fact, we humans are not very colorful. We have very subtle differences in color of our skin. We are like most mammals; most mammals are nocturnal and they are brown, tan, black or rust color, in order to be camouflaged during the day. Birds and reptiles are diurnal - active during the day, and they show bright colors. A pair of Stellar Jays migrated from the higher elevation in the Rocky Mountains to the spruce tree outside my window this winter. No human being is so beautifully blue like these birds. No human shows the intricate, iridescent colors of butterflies or the shining reflections of a gold fish. Even most of our clothes are dull. I am writing this wearing black pants, a faded grey sweatshirt, my hair is grayish and my skin is the color of concrete of the sidewalk outside. What are you wearing? What color is your skin? Are you as beautiful as blue morpho butterflies, gold fish or cardinal birds?

So why are we so obsessed about color of someone's skin? Skin is really, after all, only skin deep.

In the erotic love poem, the Song of Solomon, the dark skin of the the lover is described as lovely:

> [5]*Dark am I, yet lovely, daughters of Jerusalem, dark like the tents of Kedar, like the tent curtains of Solomon.* [6] *Do not stare at me because I am dark, because I am darkened by the sun.*

The New Testament was written during the Roman area. The Roman empire extended from the British Isles, where people would be light colored, to Africa, where people would be dark colored. The color of skin did not seem to make any difference because it was not remarked upon.

In Acts 10:34-35, Peter interacts with the crowd:

*Opening his mouth, Peter said: "I most certainly understand now that God is not one to show partiality, but in every nation the man who fears Him and does what is right is welcome to Him."*

In Galatians 3:28, Paul states:

*There is neither Jew nor Greek, there is neither slave nor free man, there is neither male nor female; for you are all one in Christ Jesus.*

In Acts 8:26-39, Phillip encounters an Ethiopian eunuch. He is identified as being a eunuch and a high official from Ethiopia. No remark or surprise about the color of his skin — this was not important.

In Europe, the color of skin was also historically not very important. The monk Saint Aidan of Lindisfarne (died 651) is credited in restoring Christianity to Northumbria in the British Isles after the fall of the Roman Empire. He was a black man. So, if you are British descent, your ancestors may have been converted by him. Abram Petrovich Gannibal was an African child adopted into the Russian royal family. His descendants married into various European royal families. So, if you are European royal, you may be related to him.

The American preoccupation with race undoubtedly arises from guilt of slavery in our country. We need to acknowledge the evil and history of slavery and only think about the color of skin when we admire the diversity of our fellow humans living on this planet.

**Color of water**

Some of my research involved studying water under extreme conditions. In one case, we studied organisms that could live below the freezing point of water. They survived subzero temperatures by producing a protein that inhibit water from freezing within their bodies. This protein is called antifreeze protein. To study this protein, I used spectroscopy, which is an experimental technique that sees how light of different color interacts with matter. While doing these experiments, I coincidentally read the book "The Color of Water: A Black Man's Tribute to his White Mother" by James McBride. McBride is biracial; his mother was white and Jewish, while his father was a black Christian pastor. He was raised in the black community and in the Christian faith. When he began to have questions about race, he asked his mother what color God is.  She answered that God is the color of water. His mother was telling him that God does not discriminate against people on the basis of color.

**Chapter 11**

# Bible Anatomy

The Israelites believed that blood contained a person's soul, as was described in Chapter 5. The symbolism of blood is constant throughout the Bible. In Chapter 9, the word eye refers to the organ that lets us see, but seeing can mean "understanding" too.

The view of the function of other body parts also differ from ours or have a deeper meaning. In this chapter, I will not quote the scriptures, but will refer you to the references in the Bible. Each of the topics below could be a separate chapter, and I leave it up to you whether you want to look into one particular subject in more detail.

### Heart

When I asked my three year-old neighbor, where she was, she pointed to her heart. The heart is moving inside us all the time, and if we think about it, we can feel it. The heart beats faster when we are excited. We die when it stops. It is no wonder that ancient people put so much emphasis on the heart.

William Harvey, in 1628, described the function of the heart as a pump. At the time, physicians thought that lungs moved blood throughout the body and I think that it must have been exciting for Harvey to realize what the function of the heart was. The idea that the heart pumps blood caused quite a stir. After all, the Bible mentions the heart 725 times in the Old Testament and 105 times in the New Testament, but never is the word used to denote the actual function of the organ as we know it.

Instead, the heart is used <u>symbolically</u> to represent what makes an individual function. The heart is used in the place of an individual's personality, intellect, memory, emotions, desires, and will.

The heart is at the center of all that we do or don't do. Heart remains at the center of many English idioms. "Good heart" is used to describe a person who is kind and generous. "Hardened heart" refers to obstinacy. "Heavy heart" means the person is sad. "Heart's desire" means something you want very deeply. "To break someone's heart" means to cause someone very strong emotional distress and sadness. "Heart-felt" means deeply sincere. These idioms have things that are common with the use of heart in the Bible. Here are a few of the 830 verses about heart in the Bible.

Exodus 8:32

Psalm 51:10

Colossians 3:23 (about work)

Proverbs 6:16-19. This passage manages to describe five body parts.

Matthew 6:21

Philippians 4:7

**Arms**

Arms can refer to the upper appendage on a body— as in "I broke my arm".  If you say that someone put his arms around you, it indicates an act of comfort and affection. Arms can also refer to weapons. At the time of the Bible, spears and swords would be formidable weapons, requiring strength in the arms. The equivalence of arms to weapons led to words army and armament.  Read these passages and consider the meaning of arms:

Deuteronomy 33:27

Luke 1:51

John 12:38

Mark 10:16

### Ears

Hearing allows us to listen to another persons talk. Hearing also can alert us to danger. We get enjoyment from hearing music. Many times music is referred to in the Bible. We do not know what the music sounded like, but it would have been the same quality that we have. Hymns that we sing date back hundreds of years and perhaps even to the second and third century.

The Bible also uses the word to mean spiritual ear — to be receptive to the word of God.

Psalm 40

Proverbs 18:15

Matthew 11:15

2 Timothy 4:3

### Face

Several times "face" in the Bible means just that — face. See Matthew 6:17-18, for example.

But it can also mean "presence" . "God's face" can mean "God's presence". There are many examples of God's face written in the Bible. Here are a few.

Genesis 30:17-23.

Number 6:24-26 These beloved verses are used as a benediction in many church services.

Psalm 80:19

Psalm 27:9

A google search reveal that there are 67 times when **"Face of the earth"** was used in the Bible. I was surprised by the frequency. Our face is the flat part of our head. Perhaps the expression arose because the earth was considered flat, and perhaps the ground underneath would be seen as round, like the back of our head. In some Bible translations, the term "face of the land" and "ground of the land" is used.

Genesis 1:25

Genesis 2:6

Genesis 7:4

Exodus 10:5

The following passage was quoted in Chapter 10. Read again and consider what "face" means:

Numbers 6: 24-26

**Feet**

The major means of transportation would be walking. The Israelites walked from Egypt to the Promised Land. Donkeys were probably used for longer distances but walking was a reliable form of transportation. In Hebrews 12: 1-2 the life of a Christian is likened to an endurance race. Here are verses on walking.

Genesis 3:8

Genesis 17:1

Leviticus 26:12

Deuteronomy 6:4-9

Psalm 82:15

Ephesians 6:15

Hebrews 12:1-2

**Hands**

The word "hand" appears about 1,800 times in the Bible. Over one-third of those times refer to the physical organ that is at the end of the arms. The other times, "hand" is used figuratively to represent the work a person does. The hands do what you want them to do, therefore they reflect the will and wishes of the entire person.

Most jobs during Bible times required the use of a person's hands. Hands are very important for many of our tasks today., even if our particular job might not require use of them. I broke a wrist several years ago and found that out without two hands I could not even properly shampoo my hair or turn the steering wheel of the car.

Hands are used to do either good or evil. Therefore, their actions are important.

Ecclesiastes 9:10

Colossians 3:23

Isaiah 35:3

**Teeth**

The Bible descriptions of teeth have entered into the English language as idioms.

"Gnashing of teeth" refers to great anguish. Teeth that "are set on edge" means great irritation and annoyance. "The Skin of Our Teeth", a witty 1942 play by Thornton Wilder, is about the possible extinction of the human race, and the idiom means a near miss. "The skin of our teeth" is a Hebrew idiom too, meaning a close call. Its origin is in Job 19:20.

Teeth have different meanings in these passages. What are their meanings?.

Job 19:20,

Jeremiah 31:29

Ezekiel 18:2,

Psalm 3:7

Job 16:9

Acts 7:54

Many idioms in English come from the Bible. Sometimes, the idioms are changed a bit. An American idiom is "It's no skin off my teeth", which means that the situation is not of much concern or danger to you. Sometimes an idiom is not in the Bible but does express a sentiment of the Bible. For instance, "Cleanliness in next to Godliness" is not in the Bible, but the Bible does have a constant theme of purity and cleanliness. Detailed instructions are given in Leviticus regarding when a person was unclean. Chapter 4 talked about baptism.

**The whole body**

I taught medical students biochemistry. During the middle of our course, the students started their anatomy course. It seemed to me, that the students changed with this experience. There was a deeper understanding of what they were doing in becoming a doctor. It is a wondrous thing to think how the organs of our body work together to maintain life.

The apostle Paul uses the whole body as an analogy to the church. Just as we need all our body parts, all of the members of the church contribute to its well-being. 1 Corinthians 12:14-26:

*14 Even so the body is not made up of one part but of many. 15 Now if the foot should say, "Because I am not a hand, I do not belong to the body," it would not for that reason stop being part of the body. 16 And if the ear should say, "Because I am not an eye, I do not belong to the body," it would not for that reason stop being part of the body. 17 If the whole body were an eye, where would the sense of hearing be? If the whole body were an ear, where would the sense of smell be? 18 But in fact God has placed the parts in the body, every one of them, just as he wanted them to be... there are **many part**s, but one body.*

Paul is emphasizing that we are a part of a congregation of believers. An ear is useless by itself. Likewise, by ourselves we are useless too. People have different skills and talents. All contribute to the work of God.

### Chapter 12

# Light and Darkness

**Seeing**

Much of what we learn in science — and in life, actually — comes from seeing things. In the Bible, light is a key symbol. The importance of light to understanding is summarized in Ephesians 5:13:

*But all things become visible when they are exposed by the light, for everything that becomes visible is light.*

Light is a symbol of knowledge and understanding in the Bible. We are going to describe how we think that light interacts with small things — atoms and molecules. And then we will summarize what we know of the biggest thing — the universe, through light. We are going to end in the same situation that the Bible writers ended: in wonderment, and knowledge that the basic workings of the universe remain unknown to us.

**Light and darkness in the Bible**

The first words of the Bible, in Genesis 1, are:

*¹In the beginning God created the heavens and the earth. ²Now the earth was formless and empty, darkness was over the surface of the deep, and the Spirit of God was hovering over the waters. ³And God said, **"Let there be light," and there was light**. ⁴God saw that the light was good, and **he separated the light from the darkness**. ⁵God called the light "day," and the darkness he called "night."*

The **first** act of God in creation as told in Genesis 1 is the formation of light — "Let there be **light**". In the Bible, light is often associated with the presence of God. The view in the Bible is that light exposes evil and sin and removes falsehood and deception.

The second act of God is sometimes overlooked. The **second** act of God is to separate the light from darkness. The overarching symbolism throughout the whole Bible is that darkness represents evil. From the very beginning, the Bible writers contrast light and darkness.

The view that light and darkness are separate forces arises from the scientific thought of the time. People observed that when the sun went down in the evening the world gradually darkened until objects could not be seen. Before the sun rises

181

in the morning, the world around them gradually becomes brighter. The very reasonable view from the Bible writers is that there was a competition between light and darkness. One would push out the other. Both light and darkness were <u>something</u>.

I think about this when I walk the dog in the morning. Doggy and I go out early, just when it is beginning to get light. By the time we get home, the sun is just rising and it is light. I like the feeling that light pushed out darkness. Ancient people can be excused for thinking light and darkness compete for each other because light precedes the appearance of the sun above the horizon in the morning. It was not until the 9th century that the Persian mathematician Abu Al-Khwarizimi calculated the height of the atmosphere and we know that the atmosphere scatters light from the sun.

The idea that light and darkness are competing is not our current view of light. Darkness is the absence of light. Light is something, but darkness is the <u>absence</u> of something — nothing.

Darkness is equated with misery and adversity in the Bible. The prophet Isaiah warns people who sin with this future:

*Then they will look toward the earth and see only distress and darkness and fearful gloom, and they will be thrust into utter darkness (Isaiah 8:22).*

Similar words are echoed by the Prophet Joel.  In Joel 2,2:

*Let all the inhabitants of the land tremble; For the day of the Lord is coming, For it is at hand A day of darkness and gloominess, A day of clouds and thick darkness, Like the morning clouds spread over the mountains.*

The dark future is changed by Christ.  Paul says in Ephesians 5: 8-14:

*For you were once **darkness**, but now you are **light** in the Lord. Live as children of light (for the fruit of the light consists in all goodness, righteousness and truth) and find out what pleases the Lord. Have nothing to do with the fruitless deeds of darkness, but rather expose them. It is shameful even to mention what the disobedient do in secret. But everything exposed by the light becomes visible—and everything that is illuminated becomes a light. This is why it is said:"Wake up, sleeper, rise from the dead, and Christ will shine on you."*

In John 8:12:

*Then Jesus said, "I am light to the world, and those who embrace me will experience life-giving light, and they will never walk n darkness."*

Therefore, the Christian belief is that like light chases away darkness, Jesus chases away evil.

The conflict between light and darkness is recorded in Gospel of John 1:5:

*The light shines in the darkness, and the darkness has not overcome it.*

1 John 1:5-7 the emphasis is that the light of God enables us to have fellowship with each other:

*This then is the message which we have heard of him, and declare unto you, that God is light, and in him is no darkness at all. If we claim to have fellowship with him and yet walk in the darkness, we lie and do not live out the truth. But if we walk in the light, as he is in the light, we have fellowship with one another, and the blood of Jesus, his Son, purifies us from all sin.*

**What is our current thinking about light interaction with matter?**

Richard Feynman, the great physicist, Nobel prize winner and teacher *par excellence* said in the introduction to his book "QED: The Strange Theory of Light and Matter":

What I am going to tell you about is what we teach our physics students in the third or fourth year of graduate school... It is my task to convince you not to turn away because you don't understand it. You see my physics students don't understand it... That is because **I don't understand it. Nobody does.**"

So, don't worry if not everything is understandable in the following description.

Light is formally called electromagnetic radiation. Visible light — light that we see — is a small part of the total electromagnetic spectrum. The study of light, and the whole electromagnetic spectrum is called spectroscopy.

Light is oscillation of an electric field and this oscillation is a form of energy. The difference between blue light is the frequency of this oscillation. The frequency range shown on the spectrum is $10^{24}$ (1 with 24 zeros after it) to 1 cycles per sec. For visible light, in analogy with music, if blue is middle c on the piano, then red is high c. We see about an octave of light. It is humbling to think that most of what there is to see, our eyes cannot see. We hear a greater frequency range of sound. The frequency range of the electromagnetic spectrum is very large whereas we see very little of the whole range of the spectrum. But we use and are affected by all frequencies.

Our thinking about light and matter is: **All matter - molecules and atoms - interact with ligh**t.

As matter interacts with light, light is changed in some way — some of its energy is transferred to matter. And matter is mutually changed by light — it now becomes more energetic.

One type of high energy electromagnetic radiation is x-rays. X-rays bounce off matter in such a way that reflects the position of atoms. This technique is called scattering. Low energy electromagnetic radiation includes radio-waves. Matter absorb radio-waves, and the absorption of one atomic group is affected by neighboring chemical groups. In this way, the relative position of atoms can be determined. You are probably familiar with the use of x-rays and radio waves. X-rays are also used to determine whether we have a broken bone. Radio-waves are used in MRI, which is used to tell if there is an abnormality in soft tissue. Microwaves is another frequency range that is commonly used. Water absorbs electromagnetic waves in the microwave range. Absorbing energy in this range makes water get hotter. That is why putting your coffee cup into a microwave oven heats up your coffee.

## Quantum levels and Uncertainty principle

Now is where, in Feymann's language, things become strange. It turns out that only certain frequencies of light absorb. When visible light impinges on a molecule, its electrons rearrange. The molecule's electrons are in now in different, but distinct locations. The molecule is said to be excited. The energy level between the two locations is distinct. That is why your red parka worn in Minnesota in winter at -40 F is the same color as when it is in Death Valley in the summer at 130 F (should you be so silly as to wear your parka in Death Valley in the summer).

The molecule absorbs light, but it is unstable, and then the electrons return to the starting position. If they do this fast, relative to the speed of light, the frequency (color) will be **uncertain**. This is somewhat analogous to the shift in frequency that you hear in a train whistle when it is moving. If you don't know whether the train is coming or going, you will not know the actual frequency of whistle.

Some philosophers and theologians have made a big kerfuffle about the "uncertainty principle", asking how does God control everything if there is something unknown and unknowable. A colleague of mine is a professor from a country who was formerly communist. During the Soviet time he was criticized for teaching physics students about the Uncertainty Principle, because, in communism, everything was supposed to be determined. I do not buy applying this principle to cases outside of the physics realm. We are <u>certain</u> about the uncertainty. We understand why there is uncertainty. Likewise, advanced physics also states there is an uncertainty in time, in theory advanced by Albert Einstein.

### How do we know what molecules are?

My scientific background is biochemistry. When I was learning chemistry, we taught to recognize the shapes of molecules. When I hear the word "water" I see the shape of the water molecule in my mind.

Water molecule has only three atoms — one oxygen and two hydrogens. Oxygen has a molecular weight of 16 and hydrogen has a weight of 1, therefore the molecular weight is 18. Each water molecule is very small. A single drop of water, as is used in baptism by sprinkling, contains approximately 2,200,000,000,000,000,000,000 water molecules. Water is very stable, and water that evaporates from one part of the world gets transferred to another area by rain or snow. No need to get water from the Jordon River for baptism. Water molecules that were used to baptize Jesus are likely to be in water that you get from the tap.

We are now in a world-wide struggle against the coronavirus Covid 19. The major protein on the outside of the virus is called the Spike protein. This is the protein which attaches to our cell outer membrane, allowing the virus to get inside our cell and then to duplicate, causing illness. The Moderna or Pfizer vaccine contains m-RNA, which goes inside of our cells, and provides the template to makes the Spike protein, without making the whole virus. The presence of Spike protein initiates an immune response in our body and gives us resistance to the virus. The number of atoms in each spike protein approaches about 176,000.

The coronavirus is spherical with protuberances. Each protuberance contains 3 Spike proteins, i.e. 528,000 atoms. The coronavirus has multiple protuberances. The shape of the entire virus and positions of millions of atoms has been determined by scientists. It is a stellar technical achievement to know the shape of the virus and positions of even each atom, among millions or even billions. This knowledge is used to design drugs that counteract the virus.

### Light in astronomy

The number of atoms in a particle such as the coronavirus is astronomical but we can find their positions by use of spectroscopy. The number of stars in the sky is astronomical — by definition! — and we also learn about them by light. We are amazed of the number of stars in the sky when we see them on a moonless, clear night. Similar amazement was express in the Bible. When God told Abraham that he would have many offspring, he said in Genesis 15 :

> *⁴Then the word of the Lord came to him: "This man will not be your heir, but a son who is your own flesh and blood will be your heir." ⁵He took him outside and said, **"Look up at the sky and count the stars—if indeed you can count them."** Then he said to him, "So shall your offspring be."*

We reside in the galaxy called the Milky Way. In 2013 the satellite Gaia was launched to map the positions of these stars. Data from the satellite allowed relative positions, the speed, and the direction of motion from one billion (1,000,000,000) stars to be determined and each star to be named. If you want a star named for your favorite aunt, say, who has everything, you can do so. I checked the cost on-line:

$34.90. You can specify a star that is seen in her area, so that she can look up at it.

A billion is a very large data base. The Milky Way Galaxy contains an estimated 100 billion stars, so about 1% of the stars in the galaxy are located and named.

The Milky Way is one galaxy. Galaxies are organized into groups, and our group of galaxies contains three large galaxies and perhaps 50 or more other galaxies. Our cluster of galaxies is one of many. No one knows how many galaxies are in the universe, but an estimate is 1 trillion. Multiply this by the average number of stars within a given galaxy you begin to realize what "astronomical number" means. In fact, an estimate of the total number of stars is in the range of one with 26 zeros after it.

For about the last 20 years, astronomers have been looking for exoplanets, the name for planets that circle a star not our sun. So far, about 5000 have been identified. If each of the stars of our galaxy have a couple of planets encircling them, the number of objects in the galaxy increases again. About 4% of the exoplanets so far discovered are about the size and position from their star as the earth. This reduces the number of possible earth-like planets somewhat, but, still 4% of a number one with 26 zeros after it, is still a very large number.

191

There are more types of objects in the universe than what we know. There are nebulae, quasars, pulsars, neutron stars, odd radio circles. Theoreticians predicted that there would be objects that are so dense and massive that light could not escape them. The first Black Hole was discovered, relatively recently, in 1971. The stars of the Milky Way circle around a Black Hole, and hence we do too.

**What is there that we don't know that we don't know about?**

When we read this we might be tempted to be self-congratulatory of the accomplishments of humankind. To me, it is a giant intellectual accomplishment to know what the structure of the Covid coronavirus is, or the position, speed and direction of travel of 1 billion stars.

Before I retired, I could hear students talking outside my office door. I remember one over-heard conversation in which two beginning graduate students gave their opinion that basically everything is known. They opined that we just have to characterize things to get better resolution (i.e. if the known answer is 6.2, we should be able to say that the answer is 6.2134). From what we know now we can infer that we will be able to learn <u>more</u> not <u>different</u>. Better telescopes will yield resolution of more stars. Better computer algorithms allow the structure of more molecules to be determined. Our DNA has been sequenced. Within the sequence is information to code all the proteins of our body. We should be able to learn what all the proteins in the body are, how each of us is unique, and how variations in our proteins affect our health.  We should be able to develop a better refrigerator, computer or car. More, more, even more!

I followed these graduate students during the course of their study. By the time they obtained their Ph.D. degrees, they were no longer saying that all is known. There was a realization that there are things that we do not know and don't know exactly how to know.

We do know that one failure is that there is no overarching theory to reconcile quantum theory, with theory of relativity (space and time) with one theory of everything. One theory should be able to describe all physical phenomena. Shouldn't it?

We began with the statement that all matter interacts with light, and that light interacts with all matter. When astronomers calculate the gravity of everything in the universe it does not account for the observation of formation of galaxies.

Approximately 85% of the universe is apparently "something else" — it is not matter and not electromagnetic waves. What is it? The same is true for energy. The universe is expanding more rapidly over time. What is the energy that is causing the expansion of the universe?

These are pretty big discrepancies between experiment and theory. There is something we do not know. <u>What is it</u> that does not interact with light?

So, our view of light and matter is still a mystery. The size of the universe and the origins of the universe are still unexplained.

We know a lot about the molecules and cells that make up our brain. But, what is consciousness? What is memory? These questions seem approachable and knowable, but can the brain fundamentally understand itself?

We remain in awe of the universe. Our situation is like describe in Amos 5:8;

> [8] *He who made the Pleiades and Orion, who turns midnight into dawn and darkens day into night, who calls for the waters of the sea and pours them out over the face of the land— the LORD is his name.*

In Job 38, the Lord told to Job:

<sup></sup>4 *"Where were you when I laid the earth's foundation?   Tell me, if you understand.*

5 *Who marked off its dimensions? Surely you know!   Who stretched a measuring line across it?*

6*On what were its footings set,   or who laid its cornerstone—*

7 *while the morning stars sang together   and all the angels shouted for joy?*

### Chapter 13

# Concluding thoughts. What do we not know?

### Need for humility

As children, we were taught in a dogmatic way: $2 + 2 = 4$, the earth goes around the sun, snow is made of water and so on. Teaching in a dogmatic way is one way to teach — if we were to say to our five-year old that <u>maybe</u> $2 + 2 = 4$, the child would become confused.

But some of the things that we are taught as children prove to be wrong. I remember being taught that there were 48 human chromosomes; now the number is recognized to be 46. The operating hypothesis for mountain formation is plate tectonics. In this theory, mountains form when two gigantic plates collide. The origin of mountains was known when I was a child, but not necessarily taught in schools. There was one hypothesis that the earth shrunk like a grape shrinks to become a raisin. Thereby, mountains as ridges were formed on a shrinking earth.. We were told that we use only 10% of our brain — usually this was told to us when our teachers and parents wanted us to study harder — but the current thinking is that we require all of our brain. Our views of things change when we have better or more information. But, more importantly, our views change when someone sees something in a different way, and is able to say "No, that is not how it works, this way better describes this observation." A paradigm shift in thinking occurs.

All people during all ages observed nature, and made assumptions about it. The writers of the Bible did so too. In reading the Bible, I agree with my brother that the authors used the best information that they had available. With the data that they had, it was not unreasonable to think that the earth is flat and it was not unreasonable to wonder of the origin of wind or fire. They marveled at the sky, but could not realize that the stars were suns, and that there were a billion billion stars that they could not see. They recognized the need for water, and to the best of our knowledge we still have the opinion that all life needs water. They questioned why disease and suffering occurs in the world. This is an unanswered question. They experienced war and strife and we still have no remedies.

We have problems which they did not consider. Will our use of the earth's resources limit our lives? Climate change, and misuse of the environment, is a very real threat. Just as the people of the Bible needed to change to face changing conditions, we are challenged to do so too. Advances in biology poses ethical questions, which we need to calmly and with kindness address.

We continue to marvel at the world around us. And we continue to question the nature of things, and how things work.

Will we ever know everything? That is another subject for speculation. It may be that our synapses are arranged so that in principle we cannot know everything. "Know thyself" is attributed to Socrates and this may be impossible to obtain. But God has given us a questioning mind, and we continue to strive. Our striving includes how our understanding of nature and this influences our view and description of God. We learn from how the people in the Bible strove to understand God.

# Questions and Discussion

**1. Wind**

The two symbols of the Holy Spirit are wind and fire. We did not discuss another feature of Pentecost. Following the appearance of the Holy Spirit on Pentecost, the Disciples spoke in tongues.

What do you think is the meaning of speaking in tongues? Does this have a meaning for our witness to the world?

Do you know a second, or more languages? After learning the language did you understand better and were more interested in the culture of the people using that language?

Is Pentecost meaningful in your church? Are there any traditions that your church or your family do to celebrate Pentecost?

Try reading a psalm aloud using breath control. Breath in one phrase, and out for the next phrase.

Look up the weather forecast online for tomorrow. Write it down. Then tomorrow check how accurate the weather forecast was. Do this for a week. Was the forecast reliable from day to day?

**2. FIre and Holy Spirt**

The process of metal refining is used by the writers of
the Bible to purification by God. But metal refining was not the
only process used to make an analogy with purification. Look
up the following references, write them down. Describe what
process is used.

John 15:6

Matthew 3:10-11

Matthew 3:12


**3. Downsides of wind and fire**

Read all of Acts 27.  And then read Acts 28 too.
(Notice that after all the adventures of Acts 27, the Island where
Paul was ship-wrecked had snakes!).

Rewrite or think of the adventures of Paul in Acts 27
and 28 using the style of Indiana Jones.  How would you cast
the characters if you would be making a movie about these
events?  How would you depict the action? Who would you be
— Paul?

Daniel 3 recounts the story of Shadrach, Meshach, and
Abednego and how they were thrown in a furnace because they
refused to obey the King's command to worship an idol.  Read

Daniel 3. What does this story tell about the power of God over flames of fire?

### 4. Water and Baptism

Have you experienced a crisis involving water? For instance, have you ever experienced a drought? How severe was it? Were you cautioned not to wash your car or water the lawn? Or did you live in conditions where you have to carry water for day-to-day use?

Did you ever experience a flood? Was the flood life-threatening to you? Did property damage occur? How long did it take for things to get back to normal?

Have these extreme conditions changed how you use and think about water?

On the flip side, have you enjoyed walking in a Spring rain? Smelling the fresh air after a rain? Enjoyed the cooling of rain during the heat of summer? Enjoyed the beauty of newly fallen snow?

### 5. Communion

Look at other translations of the Bible to see if the translation of events at the Lord's Supper changes your depth of understanding of communion.

How were you taught about the meaning of communion? Has your insights changed during your life? Do you feel communion is meaningful to you?

Has the celebration of communion changed in your church during the time that you remember? Have you visited other churches with communion practices different from what you were used to?

### 6. Creation and origin of life

Does the idea that there is more than one creation story, as outlined in Chapter 6, seem possible to you?

The theory of evolution has as its basis that all forms of life on this earth are related to each other.

The Bible says that we should be stewards of the earth. Does knowledge of the inter-relationship between living things alter how you treat the earth?

Do you think it is productive to talk to people about your views on evolution?

### 7. Diseases of infection

The Covid 19 pandemic brought up many ethical questions in society. Unfortunately, these questions sometimes caused animosity between neighbors and relatives. A situation occurred within my circle of friends. One mother was afraid that the vaccine was not safe for her child. The other mother had a child who was recovering from a serious disease, and her child was immunocompromised. The action of the first mother potentially influenced the health of the second child.

What are your obligations to keep yourself healthy? Do you have an obligation to yourself? What are your obligations to your immediate family? What are your obligations to your neighbors? To society in general?

### 8. Diseases of nutrition

I read on-line that the average life expectancy of religious people is about 4 years longer than for unbelievers. I did not find the original study to verify this statistic, but I think that we can expect that our faith will have an influence our health.

What religious practices help us to lead a healthy life?

Can you think of some examples where religious practices and beliefs are unhealthy? Consider your own beliefs as well as others.

Have you ever had an experience with malnutrition, either from not having enough food or having an insufficient amount of a vitamin or mineral? Iron deficiency is a common problem, leading to anemia. The World Health Organization estimates that 30% of the world's population has an iron status that is considered below normal. Vitamin D deficiency is also common among all age groups. Vitamin B12 is recommended for the elderly, because vitamin B12 is involved in the enzymes that make lipids in the brain. The thought is that vitamin B12 might help for some age related dementia. Does your doctor recommend nutritional supplements?

In Chapter 4 we followed the symbol of water as a purifier. Water is also needed for our life and another chapter could have been written about this. What does it mean to be thirsty? How are our bodies affected? What does it mean to "thirst for righteousness".


## 9. Palms

Does your church use plants and flowers for decoration? Do any of these of symbolic value?

The story of Judean Palms can be found on-line. Here is one link: https://timeline.com/methuselah-judean-date-palm-b3782ff1d731

**10. Vision**

The importance of eyes are reflected in the many idioms in English. Many of the idioms have origin in the Bible. Consider what they mean in the Bible and in every-day use.

| | |
|---|---|
| a beam in the eye | Matthew 7:1-6 |
| apple of my eye | Deuteronomy 32:10 |
| | Psalm 17:8 |
| | Proverbs 7:2 |
| | Lamentations 2:18 |
| | Zechariah 2:8 |
| an eye for an eye | Exodus 21:22-25 |
| | Leviticus 24:19-22 |
| | Matthew 5: 38-48 |
| an eagle eye | Psalm 103 |
| pull out your eyes | Matthew 18:9 |

**11. Bible Anatomy**

This chapter required you to write your own answers. Here is a bigger challenge. I chose "Science in the Bible" as a topic because science is my interest and career. Other topics could be chosen. You could write "Law in the Bible" or "Government in the Bible". The description of King Solomon's reign would certainly compose a major part of this. I wonder whether "counselor" in Isaiah 9:6 could also mean "lawyer" ? If you are a gardener or farmer you might like "Plants and animals of the Bible". If you like geology or gem stones you might write "Rocks in the Bible." Luke 19:40 would, for sure, be quoted by you. What topic would you be interested in?

## 12. Light and darkness

During Biblical times people were challenged by changing conditions. Abraham was a nomad. In Egypt the Israelites were slaves. During the times of the Joshua and Samuel people were transitioning from being nomads to living in towns. Political changes occurred. The Kingdom of Israel (Kings being Saul, David and Solomon) represented the union of the twelve tribes, but it lasted only about 70 years. After that the country was divided. The sovereignty of the two parts did not last long either, with the Northern Kingdom falling about 200 years before the Southern Kingdom. Several times the Israelites had to adjust to exile by conquering enemies and occupation by foreign powers. During the times of Jesus, people were adjusting to Roman occupation. During that time, in 70 AD the Romans destroyed the temple, never to be reconstructed.

How do we respond to changes? What are the questions that we need to address during our times? To get you started here are some:

Do you think that social media affects our view of the world? Does it affect who we vote for, and how we regard other people? Do you think older people or younger people are more swayed by what they learn from social media?

Do you think that we face moral and religious challenges due to advances in biology? What are these challenges?

We have age old challenges of famine, war and disease. For the first time in history, we have the ability to annihilate the human race. Are there any things that we can do now to insure the safety of coming generations?

## 13. Concluding thoughts

Do you think we can accurately forecast the future? Predict what human life will be like in 10 years. And 100 years.

# Scientific Glossary

**acetic acid**: "acid" in this book refers to a chemical group composed of carbon, C, and two oxygens, O. Acetic acid has this group and acetic acid molecule has a total of two carbon atoms. Acetic acid is what vinegar is made of. It is the building block of fat in the body. Its formula is shown in Figure 1.

**alcohol**: "alcohol" refers to a chemical group composed of carbon, C and one oxygen, O. The type of alcohol that is in alcoholic beverages has two carbons and it is called ethanol or ethyl alcohol. Its picture is shown in Figure 1. Grain alcohol and rubbing alcohol are other common alcohols. They contain one and three carbons, respectively.

**amino acid**:  Amino acids make up all proteins. Amino acids are compounds containing carbon, hydrogen and oxygen. The simplest amino acid is glycine, in Figure 1. Note below it is the similar to acetic acid but it has a nitrogen in it.

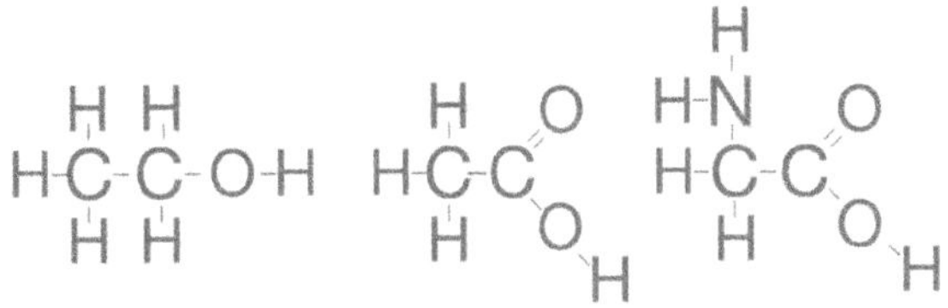

$$\begin{array}{ccc}
\text{H H} & \text{H O} & \text{H-N O} \\
\text{H-C-C-O-H} & \text{H-C-C} & \text{H-C-C} \\
\text{H H} & \text{H O-H} & \text{H O-H}
\end{array}$$

ethyl alcohol      acetic acid      glycine

Figure 1. Structures for two carbon compounds

**carbon**:      Carbon is an element. Pure carbon exists as graphite and diamonds. Carbon can be part of a vast number of compounds. It is the basis of all life forms on earth.

**carbon dioxide**: It is written as $CO_2$. A molecule of carbon dioxide is made up of one carbon and two oxygens. It is a gas at ambient temperatures. It solidifies to a solid at low temperature, to make "dry ice".

**carbohydrate**: class of compounds made up of carbon, hydrogen and oxygen. Sugar and flour are carbohydrates.

**catalyst**: A substance that increases the rate of a chemical reaction. It itself does not undergo a permanent chemical change during the chemical reaction.

**cell**:  the smallest unit of all life. Every cell is surrounded by a membrane that controls what gets in and out of the cell. Nearly all cells contain DNA, which directs how the cell makes proteins.

**compound**: substance made up by combining two or more elements. Elements are in a definite ratio within the compound.

**DNA**: deoxyribonucleic acid. It is composed of a long chain of small nucleic acid molecules. DNA contains the elements C, H, O, N plus phosphorous. There are four types of nucleic acids in DNA, abbreviated A, G, C and T. In humans, DNA is found in the nucleus of the cell.

**element**: elements make up matter. They cannot be broken down into simpler substances. There are about 100 elements.  About 11 elements are found in the human body, plus 30 or so trace elements. The elements we are considering in the Bible story are carbon, hydrogen, oxygen and sulfur.

**enzyme**: Enzyme is a catalyst in a living organism. They make reactions go faster, and by making specific reaction go faster they determine what reactions occur in the body. Enzymes are proteins.

**gene**: A gene is the basic physical and functional unit of heredity. Genes are made up of DNA. Each protein in the body is coded by one gene. It is estimated that humans have 20,000 to 25,000 genes.

**hydrogen**: Hydrogen is an element, symbol H. It is the lightest and simplest element. It has one proton and one electron. Its atomic weight is 1, by definition

**metal**: In pure form, metals are shiny, can be molded and conduct heat and electricity. Iron, copper, tin, gold and silver are all metals. Look at a diamond ring to compare pure elements that are metals and non-metallic. Diamond is pure carbon and it is not a metal; its atoms are in a crystal and it diffracts light to sparkle. The gold band is a metal. Its atoms and the electrons are not in a defined position. Light is reflected back from the surface; this occurs for all pure metals.

**nitrogen**: Nitrogen is an element. Two nitrogen atoms combine to make $N_2$, which is the nitrogen in the atmosphere. Pure nitrogen is a gas at ambient temperatures and it is the most abundant gas in the atmosphere. Its atomic weight is 14; therefore an atom of nitrogen is 14 times heavier than hydrogen. Nitrogen atoms are in all proteins.

**oxygen**: Oxygen is an element. Two oxygen atoms combine to make $O_2$, which is the oxygen gas in the atmosphere. We need oxygen to metabolize our food to give us energy. Within minutes without oxygen, we die. Its atomic weight is 16, therefore it is 16 times heavier than hydrogen. Oxygen molecules are in all proteins and carbohydrates.

**protein**: Proteins are composed of amino acids. One amino acid, glycine, is shown in Figure 1. In proteins, the amino acids are strung together in a chain. There are about 20 types of amino acids in proteins. The number of amino acids in any protein can range from the hundreds to thousands. Proteins have many functions in the body. Enzymes are proteins. Hemoglobin, which carries oxygen from lungs to tissue is a protein. Connective tissue is protein. Rhodopsin, the molecule in the eye that senses light, is a protein. Hair is protein. The substance that makes butterfly wings iridescent is a protein.

**RNA**: Ribonucleic acid. It is composed of a long chain of small nucleic acid molecules. RNA contains the elements C, H, O, N plus phosphorous. RNA is coded from DNA. RNA directs the making of proteins in the cell.

**spectrum**: Spectrum is the display of colors within a light beam. Colors differ by the wavelength of the light A rainbow shows the spectrum of colors in a beam of sunlight. In physics, spectrum refers to all the electromagnetic wavelengths, not just the wavelengths we see by eye.

**sulfur**: Sulfur is an element. In pure form it is yellow in color. Its atomic number is 32, i.e., 32 times heavier than hydrogen. It is found in some proteins within the body. Pure sulfur is called brimstone.

**sulfur dioxide**: It is a compound made up of one sulfur and two oxygen atoms. It is written as $SO_2$. It is a gas at usual temperatures. When it dissolves in water it forms sulfuric acid.

# References and additional reading

### Chapter 1

You can see the direction and speed of wind by googling "earth null school wind map". The web address is: https://earth.nullschool.net/#current/wind/isobaric/1000hPa/ort hographic=-93.41,21.48,534.

### Chapter 2

Fire is combustion; Equation 1 of this chapter is the same reaction that occurs in a gasoline powered car.

Combustion is described in simple terms on this web page from NASA:

http://www.grc.nasa.gov/WWW/K-12/airplane/combst1.html

### Chapter 3

We did not discuss how fire and wind can be harnessed to provide energy. Wind power has been used for millennia for transportation. Think how sailing on the ocean has influenced civilization. Now, we are attempting to reduce $CO_2$ emissions by getting electrical energy from wind power. Here is one book related to using wind: "Wind Power For Dummies" by Woofenden, Ian

### Chapter 4

Katherine Hayhoe, an atmospheric scientist, gives excellent, understandable descriptions of how climate change affects the earth.  Her recent book is: "Saving Us: A Climate Scientist's Case for Hope and Healing in a Divided World"

### Chapter 5

I suggest looking at the relevant scriptures.

### Chapter 6

"Evolutionary science meets evangelical faith. How teachers are helping students accept science without losing their religion" by Dean Nelson February 14, 2022, Christian Century

Neil Shubin Your Inner Fish: A Journey Into the 3.5-Billion-Year History of the Human Body. New York: Pantheon Books, 2008

The complete sequence of a human genome
SERGEY NURK  **+100 authors** *SCIENCE* • 31 Mar
2022 • Vol 376, Issue 6588 pp. 44-53

https://www.slashgear.com/831823/scientists-
decode-entire-human-genome-why-this-
matters/?utm_campaign=clip

**Chapter 7**

A. Gryzybowski, M. Nita Clinics in Dermatology,
(2016) 343-347. Leprosy in the Bible. This article gives
convincing arguments why leprosy described in the Old
Testament is not what we know now as Hansen's disease, or
true leprosy.

International        Textbook        of        Leprosy:
https://www.internationaltextbookofleprosy.
org/chapter/bioarchaeology-leprosy-learning-skeletons

Mycobacterium leprae genomes from a British
medieval leprosy hospital: towards understanding an ancient
epidemic, T.A. Mendum, V. J. Schuenemann, S. Roffey, G.
M.Taylor, H. Wu, P. Singh, K. Tucker, J. Hinds, S.T. Cole, A.

M Kierzek, K. Nieselt, J. Krause & G. R. Stewart BMC Genomics **15**, 270 (2014)


**Chapter 8: Diseases of nutrition**

Gary W. Fick. FARMING BY THE BOOK: Food, Farming, and the Environment in the Bible and in the Qurán. CSS Teaching Series No. T05-1 Department of Crop and Soil Sciences, Cornell University, Ithaca, NY 14853 USA, December 2005


**Chapter 9  Palms**

https://www.bridgesforpeace.com/article/methuselah-the-story-of-the-worlds-oldest-date-palm-tree/


**Chapter 10. Vision: a metaphor for our times**

"Reading While Black African American Biblical Interpretation as an Exercise in Hope" by Esau McCaulley, Intervarsity Press, 2020.


**Chapter 12 Light and Darkness**

If you are very ambitious, read Feymann's Lectures on Physics.